REVELS STUDENT EDITIONS

THE REVENGER'S TRAGEDY
Thomas Middleton/Cyril Tourneur

MANCHESTER
UNIVERSITY PRESS

REVELS STUDENT EDITIONS

Based on the highly respected Revels Plays, which provide a wide range of scholarly critical editions of plays by Shakespeare's contemporaries, the Revels Student Editions offer readable and competitively priced introductions, text and commentary designed to distil the erudition and insights of the Revels Plays, while focusing on matters of clarity and interpretation. These editions are aimed at undergraduates, graduate students, teachers of Renaissance drama and all those who enjoy the vitality and humour of one of the world's greatest periods of drama.

GENERAL EDITOR David Bevington

Dekker/Rowley/Ford *The Witch of Edmonton*

Ford *'Tis Pity She's a Whore*

Jonson *Bartholomew Fair* *Volpone*

Kyd *The Spanish Tragedy*

Marlowe *The Jew of Malta* *Tamburlaine the Great*

Marston *The Malcontent*

Middleton or Tourneur *The Revenger's Tragedy*

Middleton/Rowley *The Changeling*

Webster *The Duchess of Malfi* *The White Devil*

Plays on Women: An Anthology

Middleton *A Chaste Maid in Cheapside*
Middleton/Dekker *The Roaring Girl*
Anon. *Arden of Faversham*
Heywood *A Woman Killed with Kindness*

REVELS STUDENT EDITIONS

THE REVENGER'S TRAGEDY

Thomas Middleton/Cyril Tourneur

edited by R. A. Foakes

based on The Revels Plays edition
edited by R. A. Foakes and published
by Methuen, 1966

MANCHESTER
UNIVERSITY PRESS

Manchester and New York

distributed exclusively in the USA
by Palgrave

Introduction, critical apparatus, etc.,
© R. A. Foakes 1996

Published by Manchester University Press
Oxford Road, Manchester M13 9NR, UK
and Room 400, 175 Fifth Avenue, New York, NY 10010, USA
www.manchesteruniversitypress.co.uk

Distributed exclusively in the USA by
Palgrave, 175 Fifth Avenue, New York,
NY 10010, USA

Distributed exclusively in Canada by
UBC Press, University of British Columbia, 2029 West Mall,
Vancouver, BC, Canada V6T 1Z2

British Library Cataloguing-in-Publication Data
A catalogue record for this Book is available from the British Library

Library of Congress Cataloging-in-Publication Data
Tourneur, Cyril, 1575?–1626.
The revenger's tragedy / Thomas Middleton/Cyril Tourneur: edited
by R.A. Foakes.
p.   cm.—(Revels student editions)
ISBN 0-7190-4375-1 (alk. paper)
1. Revenge—Drama.   I. Foakes, R. A.   II. Title.   III. Series.
PR3172.F4   1996
822'.3—dc20

95-25044
CIP

ISBN 0 7190 4375 1 *paperback*

First published 1996
10 09 08 07 06 05 04 03   10 9 8 7 6 5 4 3

Printed in Great Britain
by Bell & Bain Ltd, Glasgow

Preface

This edition of *The Revenger's Tragedy* departs in many ways from the Revels edition that first appeared in 1966. The punctuation of the text has been modernised, and some new stage directions added to help the reader. A new Introduction takes note of recent criticism of the play, and is supplemented by a section on 'Further Reading' that outlines some of the most fruitful lines of critical inquiry into the play. The commentary on the text, which has been thoroughly revised, includes many new notes and explanations of difficulties. I am immensely grateful both to the General Editor, David Bevington, whose thorough and incisive advice has enriched the edition in various ways and saved me from many errors, and to Billy Phelan, whose checking also showed me how difficult it is to achieve consistency and get things right. I also wish to thank the editors of the Manchester University Press for their invaluable assistance.

Introduction

The Revenger's Tragedy was published without any attribution to an author after being entered in the Stationers' Register in October 1607; some copies have on the title-page the date 1607, some 1608. The first association of the play with an author appeared in a play-list published in 1656, when it was ascribed to Cyril Tourneur, possibly because of the similarity between the title and that of Tourneur's only acknowledged play, *The Atheist's Tragedy*, published in 1611. Not much is known about Cyril Tourneur's life. He served as a soldier in the Netherlands, wrote some satirical and elegiac verse, and he was connected with the stage for several years from 1611 onwards; a play by him called *The Nobleman* was acted by the King's Men in 1612, and he helped in the writing of another lost play in 1613. At the end of this year he was in government service, and probably spent a good deal of his later years abroad; he died in Ireland in 1626. One oddity about *The Revenger's Tragedy* is that it was translated into Dutch in 1618, which conceivably might suggest a link with Tourneur.[1] For a long time it was generally accepted that he wrote the play, and much effort was given to finding similarities between *The Revenger's Tragedy* and Tourneur's known writings; but in recent decades a vigorous campaign has been fought to establish Thomas Middleton as the author.

Middleton was born in 1580, and by 1602 was beginning to work as a playwright for the Lord Admiral's Men in London, on his own, and in collaboration with Michael Drayton, John Webster and Thomas Dekker. His career took off, however, with the revival at this time of the small indoor 'private' theatres in which companies of boy actors performed mainly satirical plays for audiences who could afford to pay much higher prices than were demanded at the larger 'public' arena playhouses like the Rose and the Globe. Middleton's early plays are mostly sophisticated comedies satirising aspects of life in the city, like *A Trick to Catch the Old One*, which was entered in the Stationers' Register with *The Revenger's Tragedy*, and was also printed and published by George Eld in 1608, with variant title-pages, one identifying the author as 'T.M.'. He seems to have worked as an unattached dramatist, not tied to a particular company, and after the collapse of the Children of Paul's by 1607 or 1608 he continued to write comedies for various companies of players. From about 1613 he turned to tragicomedy, and in his later years to tragedy; his best-known plays are tragedies, *Women Beware Women* (about 1621) and *The Changeling* (in collaboration with William Rowley, about 1622). From 1607 to 1616 Middleton also wrote pageants and masques for the city of London, and became its official Chronologer. He died there in 1627.

The evidence for Middleton's authorship of *The Revenger's Tragedy* is almost entirely internal, and turns on the analysis of contractions, linguistic forms, spellings and recurrent habits in phrasing. It has been shown that the play 'exhibits a distinctively Middletonian linguistic pattern found in no other dramatist of the period',[2] and the quarto of 1607–08 could have been set from a manuscript in his hand. Middleton was, for instance, unusually fond of contractions like 'I'm', 'I'd', 'on't' and 'e'en', all of which appear frequently in the text of the play. There are many other examples of Middleton's linguistic habits to be found in the text, and the play came to the printer paired with one acknowledged to be by Middleton. When he first began to write for the Admiral's Men, he was involved in writing or contributing to tragedies based on historical events, so although his main concern during the period between 1602 and 1618 or so was with comedy and tragicomedy, it is not inconceivable that he might throw off a tragedy on demand. According to the title-page, *The Revenger's Tragedy* was performed by the King's Men, presumably at the Globe, and many now think that Middleton also had a hand in Shakespeare's *Timon of Athens* (1605–06?), which was written for this company, though possibly never performed.

The play is stylistically, and indeed in other ways, quite unlike Middleton's late tragedies, *Women Beware Women* and *The Changeling*, but has links with the kind of satirical comedy he was writing for the children's theatres before 1608, and can be seen as fitting into a pattern of his development. So, for example, the character names Lussurioso and Castiza appear in Middleton's *The Phoenix* (1604), and there are some analogies between the Prince in this play and Vindice. At the same time, *The Revenger's Tragedy* seems anomalous, a brilliant *tour de force* that stands by itself as a culmination of a mode of Senecan revenge tragedy, a kind of play not otherwise attempted by Middleton. The author was familiar with earlier revenge plays, and assimilated elements from a number of them into a remarkably coherent new form. The most immediate reference is to two plays that had recently entered the repertory of the King's Men at the Globe, *Hamlet* and John Marston's *The Malcontent*. The use of a skull as a property, especially Vindice's display of it to accompany the brooding soliloquy that opens *The Revenger's Tragedy*, and the arraignment of their mother by Vindice and Hippolito in IV.iv, echoing Hamlet's denunciation of Gertrude, provide the most obvious links with *Hamlet*. In both plays a mother supposes she is to be murdered, pretends ignorance of any misdoing on her part, is persuaded to admit her guilt and resolves to live a better life. Vindice, the son of one who died of 'discontent, the nobleman's consumption' (I.i.127), is, like the hero of Marston's play, a malcontent; more generally, the frequent use of disguise, the elaborations of intrigues, the portents, appeals to heaven, the sudden comic reversals, and the self-conscious comments by characters on the rhetorical effectiveness of their lines in phrases like 'You flow well', all suggest a familiarity with Marston's play.

Both *Hamlet* and *The Malcontent* had been printed in 1604 as played by the King's Men. The author of *The Revenger's Tragedy* may have been inviting his audience to notice the connections with these plays, but he also knew other plays by Marston, whose disturbing mingling of farce, satire and tragedy in plays like *Antonio's Revenge* (1600) he develops in masterly fashion. *The Revenger's Tragedy* may also have been in some measure designed to provide the King's Men at the Globe with a play that would compare with Henry Chettle's *Hoffman* (1602), which was performed by the Admiral's Men at the Fortune, and seems to have pleased audiences there. In its opening scene, Hoffman speaks out over the dead body of his father, as Vindice soliloquises over the skull of his dead mistress; and later Hoffman, like Vindice staging his own playlet, tortures Otho, kills him, and places him in a 'cave' with the skeleton of his executed father, a scene that may have suggested the torture and murder of the Duke in an 'unsunnèd lodge' (III.v.18) by Vindice. Both plays, in turn, recall Thomas Kyd's *The Spanish Tragedy* (about 1587; published 1592, and revised with additions in 1602), in which the most famous scene shows Horatio hung in an 'arbour' and stabbed to death, as he cries 'What, will you murder me?', a line echoed by Gertrude in *Hamlet*, and by Gratiana in *The Revenger's Tragedy*, IV.iv.2.

The Revenger's Tragedy also makes use of a range of conventions common to many revenge tragedies; these include the melancholy of the protagonist, his delay in taking revenge while he overcomes scruples and works himself up into an overwhelming passion, a sense of obsessiveness or even madness in his behaviour, and the use of a masque and/or play within the play to bring about a denoue-ment.[3] Revenge tragedies of the period also often have a ghost, and in *The Revenger's Tragedy* the skull of Gloriana that figures in the opening scene and in III.v may function as the equivalent of a ghost, a grisly reminder from the past of what the revenger is driven to do. The play is not, however, merely an anthology of devices used by other dramatists; rather it may be seen as transforming its materials into something rich and strange, to mark, indeed, a turning point in the drama of the age in which it was written.

Revenge was a popular theme in the drama from the 1580s, and is a feature of much of the best-known tragedy of the Jacobean period. Why should this be so? Histories of drama may answer this question by pointing to the new availability of source materials. The plays of the first-century A.D. Roman philosopher-dramatist Seneca, which were translated in 1581, made a considerable impact on the theatre (a line from his *Hippolytus* is misquoted in *The Revenger's Tragedy*, I.iv.23). Seneca was an official at the court of Nero who experienced the intrigues, lusts and power struggles of the imperial court at first hand, and included himself as a character in his play *Octavia*, which is about Nero's treatment of his empress, who was exiled and murdered. Seneca sees power as 'the unanswerable fact in human dealings',[4] while sanctioning a philosophy of stoicism, which en-abled him to set against the cruel and arbitrary authority of the Emperor the idea that to have power over oneself is greater than to have power over others, and so validate suicide as a kind of fulfil-ment. This idea remained influential, as Hamlet and his friend Horatio, for example, are attracted to suicide, although it clashed with a Christian emphasis on patience and the need to endure suffering in this life.

At about the same time translations of French and Italian tales and histories began to appear. These filled the imaginations of writers in England with images of Italian city states as at once luxurious, cultured, full of intrigue, and, as Thomas Nashe put it in *Piers Peniless* (1592), the 'Academy of Manslaughter, the sporting place of murder, the apothecary shop of poison for all nations', where a box on the ear might be revenged thirty years later. *The Palace of Pleasure* (1567) includes the tale of a Duke of Florence who sought the help of the brother of a girl he wanted to seduce; the brother reported that he had persuaded his sister to receive the Duke in her bed, but when the Duke came there he was murdered by the brother and his servant. This episode, which suggested Lussurioso's attempt to seduce Castiza in *The Revenger's Tragedy*, has a historical basis in the murder of Alessandro de' Medici in 1537. Other intrigues in the play may have been prompted by stories derived from Giraldi Cinthio's *Hecatommithi* (1567), Matteo Bandello's *Novelle* (1554) and Guicciardini's *History of Italy*. What at first encounter perhaps seems wildly implausible in the play may thus be founded in actual events; the court in the play is not identified, but is Italianate, as indicated by the names of the characters, most of which can be explained by reference to John Florio's Italian/English dictionary, *A World of Words* (1598).

A fascination with Italy, as mythologised also in the image of Machiavelli as a representative of archetypal villainy in a country devoted to the vendetta, provided a rich background and body of source materials for Jacobean drama, but does not explain why revenge became such an important theme in the plays of this age. In Italy certain kinds of revenge were sanctioned by law, especially in those cases involving adultery, the seduction of a man's wife, or her betrayal of her husband; infidelity might be brutally punished when aristocratic honour was at stake. In England, by contrast, revenge was outlawed, for, as Francis Bacon put it in his essay on the topic, 'Revenge is a kind of Wild Justice, which the more Man's Nature runs to, the more ought Law to weed it out. For as for the first Wrong, it doth but offend the Law; but the *Revenge* of that wrong, putteth the Law out of Office.' At the same time, revenge was practised, and certain cases, like that of Sir Thomas Overbury, poisoned by the Countess of Essex in 1613 in revenge for his attempt to warn the Earl of Rochester against her, became notorious.

Here it is tempting to see an analogy with the United States and Britain at the end of the twentieth century, when television and the cinema have displaced theatre in popular entertainment. It is not long since in Britain *The Avengers* was a runaway success as a television series; and in America the common preoccupation of movies with licensed or privileged killers, type-casting actors like Charles Bronson (in the *Deathwish* series, 1974–87) or Clint Eastwood (for example, in *The Unforgiven*, 1992), or Sylvester Stallone (in *The Specialist*, 1994) to carry out revenge of one kind or another, represents and possibly fosters the idea of taking the law into one's own hands. Revenge is forbidden by law now too, but there is a common perception that we live in a corrupt society marked by extreme wealth and poverty, in which the law is too slow in taking years to punish serial killers, for example, too inefficient in dealing with street gang wars and too corrupt in allowing wealthy or powerful criminals to escape serious penalties for their crimes. James I practised and encouraged extravagance at his court, allowed or ignored increasing corruption, sold knighthoods (compare Vindice's line, 'Are lordships sold to maintain ladyships?', III.v.74), fostered the practice of selling lands in order to make a show at court (see II.i.219–26) and gave purchase to the complaints of satirists like Vindice:

> Does every proud and self-affecting dame
> Camphor her face for this? and grieve her maker
> In sinful baths of milk, when many an infant starves
> For her superfluous outside—all for this?   (III.v.84–7)

To a certain extent, then, *The Revenger's Tragedy* can be seen as exposing and satirising the extravagances and corruptions of the court of James I and city of London in the first decade of the seventeenth century. Some, like Jonathan Dollimore, would go further, and claim that the play articulates a crisis in the decay of a traditional social order in England, in the shift from feudalism to capitalism, and depicts a society stultified by the contradictions within it.[5] If there is some validity in this argument, it leaves a lot unexplained. So far as revenge is concerned, our society, like that in Jacobean London, is two-faced; while the individual's urge to retaliate is natural, our social concern is to keep this instinct in check. Both religious authority ('Vengeance is mine: I will repay, saith the Lord', Romans 12.19) and the law are established for this purpose. Our culture would like to believe 'that revenge and justice have nothing to do with each other',[6] but the problematic relationship between these two concepts has retained its fascination, and recurs as a theme in fiction, notably in detective novels, and in movies, especially Westerns and films that concern the police or the mafia.

Revenge tragedies exploit the moral tension between the desire for justice and the urge to revenge by placing their protagonists in a situation in which they cannot obtain legal redress; so Vindice enters with the skull of his mistress, poisoned by the Duke, who is himself the judge, sentencing and then reprieving Lussurioso in II.iii, and cannot be brought to justice; as he says,

It well becomes that judge to nod at crimes,
That does commit greater himself and lives.   (II.iii.124–5)

Vindice as revenger claims the moral high ground in attacking lust and luxury, but is contaminated by what, in the nine years since his mistress was murdered, has become a stored-up obsession with seeking revenge. In the course of the play he is shown taking increasing pleasure in torture and murder, as in the masque of revengers in V.iii, and in priding himself on his cleverness he becomes less morally distinguishable from the villains whose deaths he arranges.

In this respect *The Revenger's Tragedy* is concerned with an issue that is transhistorical, and is as relevant to ancient Greek society (witness the *Oresteia* of Aeschylus) as it is to the Jacobean or modern world. Critical response to the play has been largely concerned with its morality. Some dwell on the 'pervasive corruption' in the play, and see in it a vicious society engaged in a squalid quest for power, wealth and sex, in an action that springs from 'an obsessive loathing of the sexual sinfulness of men'.[7] Such readings find little sense of moral purpose at the end, while others see Vindice and Hippolito dying 'alertly, courageously, and high-spiritedly, so as to make of their deaths both a political and a moral action'.[8] An alternative reaction to the play would note that it has a clear moral structure, in which all the guilty, including Vindice and Hippolito, are finally punished, so that Vindice's cry 'Heaven is just' (III.v.187), the sound of thunder as the voice of heaven at IV.ii.202 and at V.iii.41 SD, and Antonio's line 'Just is the law above' (V.iii.91) all confirm a sense of appropriate retribution on those who have done wrong; at the same time, Vindice's 'self-abandonment to theatricality inherent in the revenger's role'[9] causes a kind of moral disorientation, since he behaves as if he were the moral spokesman in the action.

The denunciations of sin in the play are countered by the pleasure characters take in acting out or watching adultery, incest and murder. The effect may be seen as an aesthetic rather than a moral disorientation, since the play 'insists that the violence of its action be regarded not only as a representation in the theater but also as an implication . . . that the theater is a proliferation of identities, a multiplication of the self', a proliferation that disturbs the drive for moral certainty.[10] So in the masque of revengers in V.iii all the revengers look the same, and could substitute one for another; they are all versions of each other, all actors indistinguishable from other

players. It is disconcerting that women in particular represent both
an ideal of virtue (as Castiza typifies chastity) and a source of
corruption and contamination ('were't not for gold and women,
there would be no damnation', II.i.257–8); Vindice at once over-
values them and is disgusted by them. Similarly, the same bodily
action, a kiss, can be both spiritual, the mark of honourable love, as
when Vindice and Hippolito kiss their repentant mother in IV.iv,
and at the same time 'the grossest of bodily contacts',[11] as when the
Duke kisses the skull at III.v.146 and Spurio kisses the Duchess at
their incestuous meeting at III.v.207, crying, 'Had not that kiss a
taste of sin, 'twere sweet'. Here a link with *Hamlet* may be seen, but
also a marked difference. Hamlet's disgust with Gertrude is rooted
in past events; by contrast, the opening soliloquy of *The Revenger's
Tragedy* dwells entirely on the present moment, and it has been
noted that 'now' is the most frequent adverb in the play.[12] Opposing
values and paradoxical attitudes simply exist in a context of urgent
movement forward in time, 'Nine coaches waiting,—hurry, hurry,
hurry!' (II.i.206).

The moral impact of the play in its own time may be reflected in
some measure in the *Poems Sacred and Satyrical* (1641) of Nathanael
Richards, in which there are many passages alluding to or plagiaris-
ing from *The Revenger's Tragedy*. One play by Richards survives, a
tragedy, *Messalina* (printed 1640), on the adultery of the Roman
empress with her lover Silius, which, like his verse, is concerned with
'sexual temptation, its potential destructiveness, and the impossi-
bility of successfully resisting it without the timely intervention of
divine grace'.[13] In his poems Richards seems tormented at once by
his own lusts and his anxious need to deny them, as when he cannot
help staring with desire at the exposed breasts of a woman in the
audience at a play. His Protestant faith demands of him a self-
discipline he cannot sustain adequately, and he focuses his desire
and loathing in the image of women, as he tries to frighten sin out of
himself, his favourite allusion being to Vindice's address to the skull
of Gloriana in III.v:

> It were fine, methinks,
> To have thee seen at revels, forgetful feasts,
> And unclean brothels; sure, 'twould fright the sinner,
> And make him a good coward . . .   (III.v.90–3)

In considering the play's own historical context we can appreciate
other resonances it had when it was first performed. Nearly all the

early revenge tragedies were written for the large 'public' arena
theatres, the only notable exception being John Marston's *Antonio's
Revenge* (1600), which gave the Paul's Boys, a children's company at
a 'private' indoor small theatre, a chance to parody and provide a
sophisticated critique of the genre. In other words, revenge plays up
to and including *The Revenger's Tragedy* (for example, Kyd's *The
Spanish Tragedy*, Marlowe's *The Jew of Malta*, Shakespeare's *Hamlet*
and Chettle's *Hoffman*) appealed to a popular audience. One reason
for this may be that they are all set in foreign countries, chiefly
Catholic ones, like Italy and Spain (*Hamlet* is unique in its location
in Denmark), so that the corruption, lust and murder depicted
could be viewed as peculiar to places other than Protestant England.
The ostensible settings are usually unstable courts where intrigue
flourishes and the protagonists are typically characters who have lost
their place at court, or are in some way outsiders who find a means
to worm their way back into favour, and carry out their revenge.
Superficially the ambience these plays suggest has little to do with
daily life in London; *The Revenger's Tragedy*, however, though set
nominally in Italy (I.i.113), frequently, by direct address or by
implication, draws in the audience and makes them a party to the
corruption it depicts.

If *The Revenger's Tragedy* is morally unsettling, it is equally unsettling in its political and its social aspects. For if in one way it
confirms popular English prejudices about themselves in relation to
foreigners, in another way, as noted above (p. 6), it exposes contradictions in the prevailing ideology. In this respect the play is
innovatory, for the author brings together ideas and conventions not
only from earlier revenge plays, but from the satirical city comedies
like those Middleton had been writing for the children's companies.
Furthermore, the play exploits the self-conscious dramaturgy of
John Marston's plays, as in *Antonio's Revenge*, in which characters,
with an element of self-mockery, comment on themselves as boy
actors performing a play, ranting in roles too big for them, or, for
example, 'sit and talk as chorus to this tragedy'. In *The Revenger's
Tragedy* Vindice, as many have remarked, is consciously theatrical,
as contriver of plots and writer of his own scenarios, so that it seems
natural for him to come out with statements like, 'When the bad
bleeds, then is the tragedy good' (III.v.205). But Vindice, as pre-
senter of his own intrigues and plays within the play, goes much
further than this in turning on the audience, and including all his
spectators in his diatribes against vice and folly. This begins in his

opening soliloquy, when he points the skull of the dead Gloriana at the audience as a *memento mori*:

> Advance thee, O thou terror to fat folks,
> To have their costly three-piled flesh worn off
> As bare as this . . .   (I.i.45–7)

As the play proceeds, his general attack on luxury, ambition and lust is expressed often in rhyming couplets and one-line maxims, such as:

> In many places, tut, this age fears no man;
> *'Tis no shame to be bad, because 'tis common.*   (II.i.117–18)

His commentary builds then to more sustained passages such as might make a Jacobean audience squirm:

> Now 'tis full sea abed over the world;
> There's juggling of all sides. Some that were maids
> E'en at sunset are now perhaps i' th' toll-book.
> This woman in immodest thin apparel
> Lets in her friend by water; here a dame,
> Cunning, nails leather hinges to a door
> To avoid proclamation; now cuckolds are
> A-coining, apace, apace, apace . . .   (II.ii.136–43)

When Hippolito applauds Vindice's speech, 'You flow well, brother', Vindice implies that he could say much more, and specifically includes the audience in his response:

> shall I tell thee?
> If every trick were told that's dealt by night,
> There are few here that would not blush outright.   (II.ii.147–9)

There is a misogynistic strain in the way Vindice often focuses on women in his onslaught on corruption, culminating in the great central scene of the play, III.v, where he uses the skull again as an emblem in lecturing the audience:

> see, ladies, with false forms
> You deceive men, but cannot deceive worms.   (III.v.97–8)

Vindice also scourges men, however, as in his caustic comments on land-holders who sell property in order to buy a rich wardrobe for themselves and their wives, and cut a figure in London and at court, walking 'with a hundred acres on their backs' (II.i.217). The sequence in IV.ii, where Lussurioso questions Vindice in his new disguise as made melancholy by going to law, continues the attack in its images of men suing over trifling matters of property, and of the rich man 'busy threatening his poor tenants' even as he lies dying.

The insistent sense of the present moment, 'now', in the play may also give remarks by other characters a general relevance, as when Lussurioso, hiring Vindice as bawd to his own sister, says to him, 'The name', i.e. of bawd,

> Is so in league with age that nowadays
> It does eclipse three quarters of a mother.   (I.iii.156-7)

Thus, although the play may on one level confirm national prejudices in associating corruption and extravagance with an Italianate setting, on another level it frequently speaks home through various forms of direct address to a London audience. The image of a woman letting in her friend by water suggests the Thames, just as Vindice's law-talk in IV.ii refers to terms and writs that relate to the law as practised in London. When the play was first performed, the audience would surely have found in the play a general reference to the court of James I and to the city of London, as well as specific reminders for some, at any rate, of their own vices and greed. Vindice once names his dead 'betrothed lady' as Gloriana (III.v.151), which was well known as one of the poetic names by which Queen Elizabeth had been praised, notably by Edmund Spenser in *The Faerie Queene* (1590-96). Here the 'now' of the play may momentarily recall the better days of the previous reign, as opposed to the corruption and extravagance that were quickly associated with the court of James I after he came to the throne in 1603. The court in the play is marked by its gluttony, lust and addiction to revels and masques, and an audience might think of the 'palace' of the Duke as all too like that of the King in London:

> O, think upon the pleasure of the palace;
> Securèd ease and state; the stirring meats
> Ready to move out of the dishes that
> E'en now quicken when they're eaten;
> Banquets abroad by torch-light, music, sports . . .   (II.i.199-203)

The Revenger's Tragedy is unique in the masterly way it combines conflicting moral impulses with conflicting social and political attitudes. At the same time that it offers a clear moral structure, in that the guilty are punished, and the virtuous, as embodied in Castiza and perhaps Antonio, come through safely, its chief moral spokesman, Vindice, is contaminated both by the pleasure he takes in horrible revenges, as in the murder of the Duke, and in the sense of excitement his vivid descriptions of 'the pleasure of the palace' generate; he is in love with what he condemns, as perhaps the play is. At the same time that the play depicts an Italianate court, safely distancing moral and political corruption into a foreign country and enabling a London audience to feel superior to such a society, it undermines that sense of superiority by its recurrent emphasis on the here and now, by its frequent involvement of the audience as complicit in the vices depicted, and by its unmistakable implication that what is said about the court and city might apply just as well to London.

It is no wonder that many find the play unsettling, at once attractive and repellent, exciting and disturbing; and it should not surprise us that some critics have found the play to be subversive while others see it as conservative, or that some critics see moral disorientation where others find a moral structure or balance in it. The whole matter is complicated by other aspects of the play. While it is indebted to a number of contemporary plays, and reworks conventions of revenge tragedy, it also recalls the tradition of morality plays, a kind of drama that survived in various more or less sophisticated forms from the fifteenth into the late sixteenth century. The characters in such plays are usually personified abstractions, who contend for the soul of a representative of Mankind, and whose primary function lies less in their individuality than in their representative nature within an allegorical scheme portraying a struggle between good and evil. The names of most of the characters in *The Revenger's Tragedy* are equivalents in Italian of the type-names of characters in morality plays; Lussurioso represents lust and luxury, Ambitioso ambition, Castiza chastity and Vindice revenge (as he explains to Lussurioso at IV.ii.177).

The echo of the morality would suggest that the play is designed to display vice in order to denounce it and show the victory of good over evil. The vivid use of the skull of Gloriana as a death's-head shows Vindice reminding himself and the audience of the need to think upon one's end, *respice finem*; he appears like a figure from an emblem-book, or like the figure of Death itself in a Dance of Death, one of the most pervasive and powerful of moral emblems in medieval and Renaissance art. In these series Death appears usually as a grinning skeleton seizing kings, dukes, duchesses and people of every rank, as they are in the midst of the pleasures of this life. Vindice certainly presents himself as possessing a missionary zeal to 'blast this villainous dukedom vexed with sin' (V.ii.6); but, as I pointed out above, his claim to be a moral arbiter is undermined by the fact that he is excited by and comes to take pleasure in the very sins he denounces. In recalling the morality play and the Dance of Death tradition, the play at once invokes a moral scheme and characteristically undermines it.

Another feature of the play that affects response to it is its element of comedy, even farce. Early critics of the play scarcely noticed any humour, seeing in it disillusion and horror, a response summed up in a well-known essay by T. S. Eliot, who found in *The Revenger's Tragedy* 'The cynicism, the loathing and disgust of humanity ... characters which seem merely to be spectres projected from the poet's inner world of nightmare, some horror beyond words'.[14] These critics had no opportunity to see the play performed, and it was only after attending performances at the Pitlochry Festival in Scotland (1965) and the Royal Shakespeare Theatre (1966, revived in 1967 and 1969) that I appreciated the extent and importance of the comedy in the play. It is difficult, for example, from mere reading, to realise the power of the scenes in Act II where Vindice diverts Lussurioso from his aim to seduce his sister Castiza by telling him that Spurio, the Duke's bastard son, is cuckolding his father 'This night, this hour'. Lussurioso rushes on stage in II.iii with his sword drawn, ready to kill:

> Thus, and thus, I'll shake their eyelids ope,
> And with my sword shut 'em again for ever.
>   Villain! Strumpet!   [*He reveals the Duke and Duchess in bed.*]
> *Duke.* You upper guard defend us—
> *Duchess.* Treason, treason!
> *Duke.*   —O, take me not
> In sleep! I have great sins, I must have days,
> Nay, months, dear son, with penitential heaves,
> To lift 'em out, and not to die unclear.   (II.iii.6–13)

Brandishing his sword, Lussurioso draws the curtains screening the bed's occupants from the audience and himself, only to reveal, unexpectedly, his parents, the Duke and Duchess, in bed together. In a play in which 'fulsome lust' is the norm, 'uncles are adulterous with their nieces, / Brothers with brothers' wives' (I.iii.56–61), and

rape is regarded as 'sport' (I.ii.66), the author engineers a brilliant
dramatic surprise by discovering husband and wife in bed together.
For Lussurioso and the Duke it is an even greater shock, and each
is completely taken aback in a pause that can be very funny on stage.
The Duke, suddenly confronting his own death, falls into a posture
of penitence, perhaps kneeling to his own son; Lussurioso, sword
raised, and horrified to encounter his father, is paralysed, and can
say or do nothing. The Duke recovers first, as his guard, summoned
by the Duchess, enters to seize Lussurioso, who speaks truer than he
realises in saying, 'I am amazed to death', for the Duke is about to
sentence him to be executed.

Neither Vindice, who manages to slink away in the ensuing
action, nor Lussurioso, nor anyone in the audience expects that the
Duke will be in his own bed. There is comic irony in the exposure
of the Duke's hypocrisy here, as he confesses his sins at the one
moment when he is innocently occupied. The element of surprise in
this sequence is contrived by the dramatist so that the simultaneous
exposure of the Duke and Lussurioso has connections with farce.
The effect sought is quite different from the scene in *Hamlet* where
the Prince, sword in hand, comes upon Claudius at prayer for his
sins; Hamlet, like Lussurioso, is reduced to impotence, but for
reasons that arise from his character and moral uncertainties; there
is no surprise, and Claudius never knows that Hamlet was there. In
Hamlet we have the illusion that the action springs from the characters and illuminates them, whereas in *The Revenger's Tragedy* we are
invited to enjoy the theatricality of the dramatist's manipulations of
characters.

Other incidents in the play also have a comic edge to them, such
as the scenes portraying the mistaken zeal with which Ambitioso and
Supervacuo rush to bring about the execution of their Junior
Brother, while supposing they are ridding themselves of the heir to
the dukedom (III.i, iii, vi). Here the humour has a macabre quality,
as in the by-play with the 'yet bleeding head' they think is
Lussurioso's, until he enters vigorous as usual (III.vi.35–60). The
most bizarre and savage comedy energises the scene that is at the
heart of the play, when Vindice as dramaturge designs the most
theatrically satisfying staging of the death of the Duke, using the
skull of his mistress 'dressed up in tires', and inviting the audience
to share his pleasure as an artist: 'O sweet, delectable, rare, happy,
ravishing!' (III.v.1). There is macabre humour also in the way
Vindice contrives that Lussurioso, who gives the order for him and

Hippolito to stab again the dead body of the Duke, will observe them in the act of 'killing' his own father (V.i.47–71); and in the double masque of revengers, where the second group of dancers is taken aback to find those they intended to murder already dead (V.iii.40–50).

At the same time, *The Revenger's Tragedy* impresses audiences in the theatre, like its readers, as a serious drama. 'The opposed possibilities of laughter and horror are both fully realised',[15] as Nicholas Brooke points out, and what seems a contradiction may be explained by the extent to which the play offers a 'comic release from conventional moral restraints'.[16] The horror of what takes place in the action, rape, torture, murder, execution, would perhaps be unbearable were it not for the stylised and self-conscious element of grotesque comedy involved, which continually reminds the audience that they are watching a dramatic fiction. Our understanding of the nature of black comedy or tragic farce was sharpened by the encounter in the 1950s and 1960s of the English-speaking world with the theatre of cruelty, and the work of Artaud, Brecht and Beckett. The mode of *The Revenger's Tragedy* prevents the audience from a full sympathetic identification with the characters, and the play exerts something like the alienation effect Brecht sought, demanding an intellectual rather than an emotional engagement with its conscious theatrical artifice.

Although there had been a number of amateur productions in colleges and universities, the first major professional revival came with one directed by Brian Shelton at the Pitlochry Festival in Scotland in 1965, which was followed by the very successful production at the Royal Shakespeare Theatre in 1966, revived in Stratford in 1967 and in London in 1969. The director of this, Trevor Nunn, saw the play as 'extraordinarily about aspects of our own world . . . where the relationship between sex, violence and money was becoming increasingly popular, and expressed through all sorts of things—spy novels—James Bond'.[17] He saw Vindice as schizophrenic, as like modern western society, totally fascinated by what at the same time appals and demoralises. His production emphasised sexuality and cruelty, staging one scene (IV.ii) in a torture-chamber, with prisoners stretched on racks, and diminished the Christian frame of reference.[18] The decade of the 1960s gave us the 'permissive society' and the 'good life' (the programme notes included reference to Fellini's film *La dolce vita*); this decade also saw the erection of the Berlin Wall, the assassination of President Kennedy and the beginning of the war in Vietnam. A sense of possible apocalypse gave special relevance to works like Samuel Beckett's *Endgame*; if things are really so bad, perhaps the only way we can face them is as black comedy, to make some kind of game out of death itself. It would seem that since then the western world has become ever more fascinated by the pursuit of wealth, luxury, sex and violence, and at the same time horrified by the corruption of morals and devaluation of life that results. *The Revenger's Tragedy* is every bit as relevant now (as later productions by the Royal Shakespeare Theatre in 1987, and in Los Angeles in 1989 showed),[19] and as disturbing. The opposing impulses in the play retain their topicality, notably those between the fascination with luxury and vice in a world where courtiers go 'in silk and silver, . . . never braver' (I.i.52), and the appeals to religion and 'that eternal eye / That sees through flesh and all' (I.iii.65–6).

Perhaps what is most disturbing about these impulses is that they are complementary; Martin Esslin, reviewing Trevor Nunn's production in 1970 went further:

> we are shown two attitudes which are both equally perverse and which ultimately are identical; pursuit of lust for its own sake and the perverse preoccupation with the fight against the flesh which is only experienced by those who have to suppress just such lustful preoccupations. Both perverse stances are equally reprehensible and sick and we can gain the true distance to them merely by healthy laughter.[20]

This passage is, of course, based on a somewhat slanted version of the play, and is reminiscent of the preoccupations of Nathanael Richards in his reaction to the play (see p. 8 above); but it is suggestive in relation to a modern society that is hooked on the sex life of its celebrities, while thumping the Bible and preaching family values; a society, too, that is terrified of and condemns violent crime, yet delights in films of horror and bloodshed and makes deadly weapons freely available.

To do justice to *The Revenger's Tragedy* we need to take into account some other factors. The play springs to life the moment it begins through the concentrated force of its poetry, especially in the voice of Vindice. The opening is indeed brilliant, as, holding the skull of the dead Gloriana, he surveys the passage by torch-light over the stage of the Duke and his family, magnificently dressed. Vindice satirically reduces them to their moral attributes or 'characters':

> Duke, royal lecher; go, grey-haired adultery;
> And thou his son, as impious steeped as he;

And thou his bastard, true-begot in evil;
And thou his Duchess, that will do with devil;
Four excellent characters!

The play begins in rhyming couplets, and there is a good deal of
rhyme throughout; in the first act, for example, 120 out of about five
hundred lines rhyme, and Vindice especially falls into couplets that
often provide a neat summing up or generalisation, some, as at I.i.38
and 132, marked off in the text as *sententiae*, or pithy sayings worthy
to be noted. Initially these have the effect of establishing Vindice as
moral spokesman, condemning the Duke as murderer of his love;
but even as he dwells on her beauty and chastity, her face 'So far
beyond the artificial shine / Of any woman's bought complexion'
(I.i.21–2), he sees her also as a source of temptation, able to tempt
to sin 'the uprightest man'. In converting his ideal woman into a
temptress and in dwelling pleasurably on the pursuit of his revenge,
Vindice already, by the end of his opening soliloquy, shows himself
to be contaminated by what he condemns in others.

Yet Vindice is not simply reduced to the same level as other
characters who use a neat couplet, proverb, or sententious saying to
lend an appearance of justification to vicious intentions, or an aura
of time-honoured wisdom to the nasty satisfactions of lust or revenge. The Duke, Lussurioso and others are expert in parading
such utterances, which punctuate their speeches in lines like
Lussurioso's

I know this, which I never learned in schools:
The world's divided into knaves and fools;   (II.ii.4–5)

or Supervacuo's

            Faiths are bought and sold;
Oaths in these days are but the skin of gold.   (III.i.6–7)

Ambitioso caps this rhyme by saying 'In troth, 'tis true too', and
such approving comments (compare, for example 'y' have truly
spoke him', I.i.91; 'Why, well said', I.iii.160, and 'You deal with
truth, my lord', I.iv.24) reinforce the sense that characters are using
platitudes to justify their actions, or paying lip-service to a morality
they do not live by, as when the Duke momentarily becomes aware
of his own sinfulness:

Age hot is like a monster to be seen;
My hairs are white, and yet my sins are green.   (II.iii.131–2)

The next thing the Duke does is hire Vindice in his disguise as the bawd Piato, to 'greet him with a lady' to gratify his lust (III.v.12). The gap between words and actions is typical of the courtiers, whose moral capacity is limited to sententious phrases that prove to be grossly inadequate, grotesquely misapplied or relevant with an irony they do not comprehend.

Vindice is different, for although his opening soliloquy shows him to be morally confused in his perception of his dead love as at once an image of purity and a temptress, he is, for most of the play, the agent of our awareness, who satirically exploits and exposes the gap between what others profess and what they do. They are absorbed in their intrigues and jostlings for power, while Vindice, as outsider, introduced into the court by his brother Hippolito, has the cleverness to work on and manipulate others. His is the controlling voice in the play until almost the end. The disguises he puts on in order to be hired by Lussurioso, first as a bawd, Piato, and later, in IV.ii, as a malcontent (when he is, in a typically witty scene, hired to kill his old self, the bawd), enable him to deal with the Duke, Lussurioso and the rest, including his mother and sister, on their level, and probe their vices and weaknesses. In this way he discovers viciousness beyond his own imaginings, when he is hired to tempt his mother to act as pander with her own daughter:

> *Vindice.* O fie, fie, that's the wrong end, my lord. 'Tis mere impossible that a mother by any gifts should become a bawd to her own daughter.
> *Lussurioso.* Nay then, I see thou'rt but a puny in the subtle mystery of a woman; why, 'tis held now no dainty dish. (I.iii.150-4)

He then finds that Lussurioso is right in suggesting his mother will be willing to aid him in this way. Vindice can thus play the role of bawd and pander to the full, while bringing out in his incredulity, as in the passage quoted, or in asides to the audience, or a soliloquy like that at II.ii.90-105, the vicious nature of what he is about, and of the people he deals with.

In addition, Vindice can always be himself when alone with his brother and confidant Hippolito, and both may comment on the iniquities of the court. The word 'brother' echoes through the play. These two, who support one another, and their chaste sister Castiza, act together and win our confidence as spokesmen for the play; they stand in opposition to the other five 'brothers' in the play, the sons of the Duke and Duchess, who hate each other, plot against one another for the succession to the dukedom, and are given to lust, adultery, even incest (Spurio with the Duchess).[21] It is dramatically appropriate, therefore, that the central scene in the play should begin with Vindice sharing with Hippolito his second meditation on the skull of his dead betrothed. Up to this point these two have exposed the vices of the court and praised the virtue of their sister in appealing to a Christian dispensation:

> O suff'ring heaven, with thy invisible finger,
> E'en at this instant turn the precious side
> Of both mine eyeballs inward, not to see myself! (II.i.129–31)

> O angels, clap your wings upon the skies,
> And give this virgin crystal plaudities! (II.i.245–6)

> Forgive me, heaven, to call my mother wicked! (II.ii.96)

These appeals are reinforced in the first part of the play by the occasional insights of other characters into the moral nature of what they are doing, as when the Duchess, making love to Spurio, refers to the seventh commandment (against adultery) at I.ii.161, and Spurio takes pleasure in revenging himself upon his father, 'O, one incestuous kiss picks open hell' (I.ii.174); or in Lussurioso's attempt to damn Castiza in seducing her:

> Hast thou beguiled her of salvation,
> And rubbed hell o'er with honey? (II.ii.22–3)

The Christian framework of the play is enhanced by the two idealised women, the wife of Antonio, who dies with 'A prayer-book the pillow to her cheek' (I.iv.13; her suicide, recalling that of Lucretia, ravished by Tarquin, is hardly Christian, but still makes her an emblem of moral fortitude), and Castiza, who rejects her mother's attempt to persuade her to prostitute herself to Lussurioso (II.i). At the same time, Vindice successfully calls on 'Impudence, / Thou goddess of the palace' (I.iii.5–6) to enable him to be 'a right man then, a man o' th' time' (I.i.94), and be accepted as Piato, as one who shares the mores of the palace and will promote lust, seduction and murder. The play begins in torch-light; night or darkness are associated with the crimes and sins in the play. We are given the sense that feasting and drunkenness promote sin, as Spurio was begotten after 'some gluttonous dinner' (I.ii.180), and Antonio's wife was raped in 'the height of all the revels' (I.iv.37); Vindice sums this theme up in his account of fulsome lust and 'Drunken procreation' (I.iii.57), something to which he is becoming a party even as he puts it in a Christian context, 'if anything / Be damned, it will be twelve o'clock at night' (I.iii.66–7).

The revels at court, the luxury and drunkenness that provoke lust, are linked with the idea of masques and disguises. The Duchess's youngest son rapes Antonio's wife while masked (the word 'vizard' recalling the skull, 'death's vizard', that Vindice holds at I.i.50):

> Then, with a face more impudent than his vizard,
> He harried her amidst a throng of panders
> That live upon damnation of both kinds,
> And fed the ravenous vulture of his lust.   (I.iv.41–4)

Eating and drinking are associated with male lust, so that Antonio's chaste wife appears as a victim, yet women are more often the targets of Vindice's attacks. It is easy, he implies, for them to conceal their sins under the masks they wear in the daytime:

> in the morning,
> When they are up and dressed, and their mask on,
> Who can perceive this?—save that eternal eye
> That sees through flesh and all.   (I.iii.63–6)

All these threads are drawn together in the central scene, III.v. Vindice pursues his revenge against the Duke in the dark ('in this unsunnèd lodge / Wherein 'tis night at noon', ll. 18–19, until Hippolito displays a torch, recalling the opening scene, l. 148) by means of the skull of Gloriana, dressed up and masked to look like a living woman; he unmasks her (l. 48) for Hippolito's benefit, and then conceals the skull, saying 'thou hadst need have a mask now' (l. 114). The idea of a mask links the murder of the Duke with the rape of Antonio's wife and the sins of the court, in a context of feasting, revelry and drunkenness (ll. 15, 58–9, 84–92). The skull confronts the audience too, functioning as a reminder that death and punishment for sins await us all, both men who risk all, and 'put their life between the judge's lips' (III.v.77), for the sake of sexual pleasure and women:

> Does every proud and self-affecting dame
> Camphor her face for this? and grieve her maker
> In sinful baths of milk . . . ?   (III.v.84–6)

The first part of the scene, the exchange between Vindice and Hippolito, also rises to a poetic climax in Vindice's meditation on the skull, and on the expense of money, time, life itself, all for the momentary pleasure of sexual gratification:

> Are lordships sold to maintain ladyships
> For the poor benefit of a bewitching minute? (III.v.74–5)

The last part of Vindice's meditation turns a moral spotlight on the audience too, including them, and especially women, in the lesson the skull offers:

> see, ladies, with false forms
> You deceive men, but cannot deceive worms. (III.v.97–8)

Here, at the play's centre, Vindice perceives people as mad in pursuit of luxury and lust:

> Surely we are all mad people, and they
> Whom we think are, are not; we mistake those;
> 'Tis we are mad in sense, they but in clothes.
> *Hippolito.* Faith, and in clothes too we, give us our due.
>
> (III.v.80–3)

Questioning the nature of madness and sanity in this way has been a concern of the present age, and these lines strike deep. If the mad are known by their eccentric dress, their appearance, then, Hippolito suggests, 'we', the courtiers of the palace in their extravagant doublets and ruffs, and the audience too, are mad both in 'sense' for pursuing luxury and in 'clothes' for loving finery.

Yet the most incisive of Vindice's, and the play's, moral perceptions occurs at the very moment when he yields to another kind of madness in his obsession with revenge. He gloats excitedly in anticipation of another kind of pleasure, 'O sweet, delectable, rare, happy, ravishing!', and does not apply to himself the lessons he preaches to others. The appearance of the skull ought to 'tempt a great man— to serve God' (l. 55), but it is the occasion for Vindice to enjoy the ingenuity of his revenge. After the Duke enters, looking for the perverse stimulation of a 'sin that's robed in holiness' (l. 141), Vindice poisons him in an act that forces him to recognise that he has put himself on the same moral level as those he denounced. When the dying Duke asks, 'What are you two?', Vindice replies revealingly, 'Villains all three!' (ll. 153–4). Gloriana died rather than submit to the embraces of the Duke, so that, in using her dressed-up skull as his means of revenge, Vindice becomes a kind of bawd in urging the Duke to kiss her, and in a sense prostitutes her to the Duke, as Hippolito jokingly indicates when he removes his hat to 'stand bare / To the Duke's concubine' (ll. 41–2),[22] not knowing at that point what 'lady' Vindice would produce.

In aligning himself here with the other villains in the play, Vindice effectively undercuts his own moral stance and implicitly brushes off any concern with the possibility of life after death and punishment for sins. There is a double irony in his call for thunder, the biblical voice of God, to punish Lussurioso at IV.ii.202, and his delight when he actually hears thunder (V.iii.41 SD), for, on the one hand, he does not notice that it might signal punishment for him just as much as for Lussurioso and the court; and, on the other hand, in relation to the action as a whole, the thunder has little significance, as does the blazing star seen by Lussurioso and the nobles at V.iii.15–17. Whatever verbal homage most of the characters occasionally pay to religion, it has no effect on their actions, and it is never clear that any but Castiza and her repentant mother in IV.iv really behave as if an 'eternal eye' is watching them. Because it was an age in which the fear that there might be nothing but oblivion beyond death exerted considerable pressure, in revenge tragedy, 'Mortality becomes conveniently externalized and localized in a villain . . . Revenge tragedy offers a figurative way of saying (with Donne), "Death, thou shalt die"; isolating the source of mortality in a human villain is a fantasy that cures the passivity and futility of mourning.'[23] So Vindice and Hippolito at the end are untroubled by thoughts of divine retribution, and go off boasting of the murders they have 'wittily' carried out.

The death of Lussurioso is contrived by Vindice appropriately in a masque, in which he and Hippolito and two other lords have suits made identical with those being fashioned for other nobles who plan to entertain Lussurioso at his installation as Duke. Vindice does not know that this group of four nobles includes Lussurioso's brothers, or that they are planning to murder him. Dramatically the scene in which two groups of masquers dance in, one after the other, is a stunning way of arranging the deaths of all the sons of the Duke and Duchess. It has wider resonances too in making a scene of revels bring about their deaths, and in the visual identity of the masquing costumes, for the masquers are indistinguishable one from another, so that Vindice and his brother become look-alikes of the other courtiers. All are playing roles, putting on disguises, trying to outsmart the rest for the sake of power and pleasure. One reviewer of the 1987 production at the Swan Theatre in Stratford found that she expected at the end 'to see the "true" self', as in the last soliloquy of Shakespeare's *Richard III*, 'but there is no such person, and thus no sense of closure'.[24]

Vindice gains no insights into himself, but ends as he began, cleverer than the rest, as a master of disguises and intrigues. Castiza, who alone remains an emblematic figure of virtue, resisting her mother's blandishments, appears in only two scenes, and, in the context of the whole play, her concern to preserve her 'virgin honour' (II.i.194; IV.iv.152) isolates her from everyone else. Vindice's image of her sitting 'at home in a neglected room, / Dealing her short-lived beauty to the pictures . . .' (II.i.213–14), seems to anticipate her future as an impoverished, lonely old maid. In a play-world that offers no alternative, the most memorable passages of verse employ the energy of their restlessly active images to suggest the excitements of the luxury and pleasures of the court, as when Vindice tries to tempt her:

> Banquets abroad by torch-light, music, sports,
> Bare-headed vassals that had ne'er the fortune
> To keep on their own hats, but let horns wear 'em;
> Nine coaches waiting,—hurry, hurry, hurry!
> *Castiza.* Ay, to the devil.   (II.i.203–7)

Castiza is the only one worrying seriously about the devil. The rest have their eyes on the court and its pleasures; and when a wrong is done to them, they do not leave vengeance to God, but seek their own revenge, including even Antonio (I.iv.73–4), who is left to rule at the end.

The Revenger's Tragedy is fascinating and disturbing because it reveals something unsettling about the true nature of our world, that of the present day as much as Jacobean London. It shows us a society for which Christianity provides a convenient frame of reference to remind themselves and us of good and evil, sin and divine punishment, heaven and hell, but it is, in truth, a society that pays only lip-service to such concepts and is in love with the pursuit of wealth, pleasure and power to such an extent that in practice Christian teaching and morality are ignored. The ruthless competitiveness of such a world breeds corruption and violence, so that revenge becomes the only way to secure justice. The allusions to sin and hell in the play may have no bearing on the way characters behave, and the thunder and blazing star may be theatrical effects that 'carry no

Christian conviction',[25] even if they do provide a perspective through which we see the horror beneath the witty and ebullient surface of the action.

FURTHER READING

This is not a comprehensive discussion, and I refer in the main to books of particular interest published in the last twenty years, together with one or two of the most helpful articles on the play. The best account of the importance of Seneca in relation to revenge and stoicism is to be found in Gordon Braden's *Renaissance Tragedy and the Senecan Tradition* (New Haven: Yale University Press, 1987). For a wide-ranging consideration of revenge with reference to ancient and modern literatures and culture, Susan Jacoby's *Wild Justice: The Acting of Revenge* (New York: Harper and Row, 1983), is well worth consulting; it includes a discussion of Christian and Jewish attitudes to retribution and forgiveness, and a consideration of the role of revenge at the present time in western societies. Jonathan Dollimore offers a provocative and stimulating reading of Jacobean tragedy, with a chapter on *The Revenger's Tragedy*, in his *Radical Tragedy* (1984; second edition, Durham, N. C.: Duke University Press, 1993). He sees Jacobean tragedy as confronting and articulating a crisis in the disintegration of a traditional social order, and for him plays like *The Revenger's Tragedy* are radical in subverting the idea of a providential order, and in their political and social realism in demystifying the structures of power and the social order of the age of James I. Although their primary emphasis is on madness and other conventions in revenge tragedy, in *The Revenger's Madness: A Study of Revenge Tragedy Motifs* (Lincoln: University of Nebraska Press, 1980), Charles A. Hallett and Elaine S. Hallett take a more straightforward view of the social relevance of revenge plays, arguing that they relate to a society in which civilisation has broken down.

Others have found the opposite, a conservatism in revenge tragedy, especially during the reign of Elizabeth, when its depiction of foreign, and especially Catholic, rulers and courts as unstable and corrupt is likely to have been interpreted by audiences as supporting a nationalistic ideology. Wendy Griswold, whose book *Renaissance Revivals: City Comedy and Revenge Tragedy in the London Theatre 1576–1980* (Chicago: Chicago University Press, 1986) presents an argument along these lines, is principally concerned with the social and political bearings of revenge plays, and notes that even when disillusion set in with James I on the throne, plays like *The Revenger's Tragedy* continued to end with a restoration of order in the state. In *Anticourt Drama in England 1603–1642* (Charlottesville: University of Virginia Press, 1989), Albert H. Tricomi also argues that *The Revenger's Tragedy* does not reject received values, but rather shows a zealous and anti-humanistic Christian conservatism, aiming to expose spiritual blindness in the world of the court.

Much has been written on the morality of the play and its protagonist, Vindice, and whether the play is in the end positive in establishing a moral balance or affirmation, or merely cynical in making morality, if not life itself, seem futile. A thorough survey of criticism on the play up to 1975 or so, most of it concerned with morality, may be found in Charles R. Forker's essay on Tourneur in *The New Intellectuals: A Survey and Bibliography of Recent Studies in English Renaissance Drama*, edited by Terence P. Logan and Denzell S. Smith (Lincoln: University of Nebraska Press, 1977). In his book *Cyril Tourneur* (Boston: Twayne Publishers, 1977), Samuel Schuman seems to support the second position in his account of the play as transforming a divine moral order into a corrupt quest for worldly ends. A more sophisticated attempt to explain a sense of moral disorientation in his response to *The Revenger's Tragedy* may be found in Howard Felperin's *Shakespearean Representation* (Princeton: Princeton University Press, 1977); he sees Vindice's theatricality as undermining his ethical integrity, and points in contrast to Shakespeare as rejecting theatricality in order to open his plays to an ethical criticism. An incisive critique and modification of Felperin's position is to be found in Scott McMillin, 'Acting and Violence: *The Revenger's Tragedy* and its Departures from *Hamlet*', *Studies in English Literature*, 24 (1984), 275–91; this essay provides a fuller analysis of theatricality, role-playing, and their relation to identity in the play.

The play has troubled some critics who find it hard to deal with its comic or grotesque elements. Peter Mercer, in *Hamlet and the Acting of Revenge* (London: Macmillan, 1987), comes to *The Revenger's Tragedy* via Seneca and John Marston, and sees a puritanical outrage at corruption and an acute anxiety about sexuality in the play, which he cannot square with the idea of Vindice as mocking entertainer, so that he feels the play effectively abandons tragedy. In *Horrid Laugh-*

ter in Jacobean Tragedy (New York: Barnes and Noble, 1979), N. S. Brooke takes a different tack, recognising laughter and horror as both present in the play, and arguing that its stylisation allows a sense at once of order and of wild, barely contained disorder.

Anyone interested in the authorship problem and the text should consult Macd. P. Jackson's facsimile edition of the 1607/08 Quarto and his introduction in *The Revenger's Tragedy Attributed to Thomas Middleton* (Toronto: Associated University Presses, 1987).

The best idea of the effectiveness of the play in the theatre is provided by Stanley Wells's account of the Royal Shakespeare Theatre production that ended in 1969: '*The Revenger's Tragedy* Revived', *The Elizabethan Theatre VI*, edited by George Hibbard (Toronto: Macmillan of Canada, 1978), pp. 105–33. The significance of the emphasis on the body and its functions, especially eating and drinking, in *The Revenger's Tragedy*, is considered in a powerful essay by Peter Stallybrass, 'Reading the Body: *The Revenger's Tragedy* and the Jacobean Theater of Consumption', *Renaissance Drama* new series 18 (1987), 121–48. This essay also deals with the function of the women in the play. For an understanding of the play in the larger context of Elizabethan and Jacobean tragedy, Robert N. Watson's essay on 'Tragedy' offers a good current guide, in *The Cambridge Companion to English Renaissance Drama*, edited by A. R. Braunmuller and Michael Hattaway (Cambridge: Cambridge University Press, 1990), pp. 301–52; a more radical approach, with an emphasis on the construction of identity and meaning in the period, may be found in Catherine Belsey's *The Subject of Tragedy* (London: Methuen/Routledge, 1985).

NOTES

1 *Wreack-Gerigers Treur-Spiel*, as translated by T. Rodenburgh (Amsterdam, 1618); see Beatrijs de Groote, 'Nieuwe Gegevens over het Leven van Theodore Rodenburg, Contemporain Vertaler van *The Revenger's Tragedy*', in *Elizabethan and Modern Studies Presented to Professor Willem Schrickx on the Occasion of his Retirement*, edited by J. P. vander Motten (Ghent: Seminarie voor Engelse en Amerikaanse Literatur, 1985), pp. 85–95.

2 Macd. P. Jackson, editor, *The Revenger's Tragedy Attributed to Thomas Middleton: A Facsimile of the 1607/8 Quarto* (London and Toronto: Associated University Presses, 1983), p. 23; the introduction reviews the evidence for authorship fully, from the point of view of a committed Middletonian.

3 For an account of these conventions, see Charles A. Hallett and Elaine S.

Hallett, *The Revenger's Madness: A Study of Revenge Tragedy Motifs* (Lincoln: University of Nebraska Press, 1980), Chapters 1–4.

4 Gordon Braden, *Renaissance Tragedy and the Senecan Tradition* (New Haven: Yale University Press, 1985), p. 30.

5 *Radical Tragedy: Religion, Ideology and Power in the Drama of Shakespeare and his Contemporaries* (Brighton: Harvester Press, and Chicago, University of Chicago Press, 1984; second edition, Durham, N. C.: Duke University Press, 1993), Chapter 1, 'Contexts'.

6 Susan Jacoby, *Wild Justice: The Evolution of Revenge* (New York: Harper and Row, 1983), p. 12.

7 The first quotation is from p. 302 of Larry S. Champion's essay, 'Tourneur's *The Revenger's Tragedy* and the Jacobean Tragic Perspective', *Studies in Philology*, 72 (1975), 299–321. Compare Samuel Schuman, *Cyril Tourneur* (Boston: Twayne Publishers, 1977), pp. 79–100. The second quotation is from Peter Mercer, *Hamlet and the Acting of Revenge* (London: Macmillan, 1987), p. 95.

8 Jonas A. Barish, 'The True and False Families of *The Revenger's Tragedy*', in *English Renaissance Drama: Essays in Honor of Madeleine Doran and Mark Eccles* (Carbondale: Southern Illinois University Press, 1976), pp. 142–54, citing p. 154.

9 Howard Felperin, *Shakespearean Representation* (Princeton: Princeton University Press, 1977), p. 166.

10 Scott McMillin, 'Acting and Violence: *The Revenger's Tragedy* and Its Departures from *Hamlet*', *Studies in English Literature*, 24 (1984), 275–91, especially pp. 285–6.

11 See Peter Stallybrass, 'Reading the Body: *The Revenger's Tragedy* and the Jacobean Theater of Consumption', *Renaissance Drama*, new series 18 (1987), 133.

12 McMillin, 'Acting and Violence in *The Revenger's Tragedy*', pp. 282–3.

13 Citing from p. 70 of the essay by Alan T. Bradford, 'Nathanael Richards, Jacobean Playgoer', *John Donne Journal*, 2 (1983), 63–78.

14 *Selected Essays* (London: Faber, 1951), pp. 189–90; the essay was first published as a review of the edition of *The Works of Cyril Tourneur* by Allardyce Nicoll (1930).

15 Nicholas Brooke, *Horrid Laughter in Jacobean Tragedy* (New York: Barnes and Noble, 1979), p. 24.

16 Citing p. 263 of Richard T. Brucher's article, 'Fantasies of Violence: *Hamlet* and *The Revenger's Tragedy*', *Studies in English Literature*, 21 (1981), 257–70.

17 Cited by Stanley Wells, p. 107, in his excellent account of the production, '*The Revenger's Tragedy* Revived', *The Elizabethan Theatre VI*, edited by G. R. Hibbard (Toronto: Macmillan, 1978), pp. 105–33.

18 Wells, '*The Revenger's Tragedy* Revived', pp. 119, 115.

19 See the reviews by Lois Potter in the *Times Literary Supplement*, 25 September–1 October 1987, p. 1048, and by Miranda Haddad in *Shakespeare Quarterly*, 41 (1990), 120–3.

20 Cited in Wells, '*The Revenger's Tragedy* Revived', p. 125.

21 See Barish, 'The True and False Families of *The Revenger's Tragedy*', pp. 145–51.

22 Mark Gauntlett, ' "Had his estate been fellow to his mind": Ironic Strat-

egies in *The Revenger's Tragedy*', *Cahiers Élisabéthains*, 42 (1992), 37–48, especially p. 44.

23 Citing Robert N. Watson's chapter on tragedy in *The Cambridge Companion to English Renaissance Drama*, edited by A. R. Braunmuller and Michael Hattaway (Cambridge: Cambridge University Press, 1990), p. 318.

24 Lois Potter, *Times Literary Supplement*, 25 September–1 October 1987, p. 1048.

25 Watson, 'Tragedy', p. 333.

THE REVENGER'S
TRAGEDY

The Revenger's Tragedy
Act I

Enter VINDICE *[holding a skull; he watches as] the* Duke,
Duchess, LUSSURIOSO *his son,* SPURIO *the bastard, with a
train, pass over the stage with torch-light.*

Vindice. Duke, royal lecher; go, grey-haired adultery;
    And thou his son, as impious steeped as he;
    And thou his bastard, true-begot in evil;
    And thou his Duchess, that will do with devil;
    Four excellent characters! O, that marrowless age   5
    Would stuff the hollow bones with damned desires,
    And 'stead of heat, kindle infernal fires
    Within the spendthrift veins of a dry duke,
    A parched and juiceless luxur. O God!—one
    That has scarce blood enough to live upon,   10
    And he to riot it like a son and heir?
    O, the thought of that
    Turns my abusèd heart-strings into fret.
    Thou sallow picture of my poisoned love,
    My study's ornament, thou shell of death,   15
    Once the bright face of my betrothèd lady,
    When life and beauty naturally filled out

I.i.4. *do*] copulate.

5. *excellent characters*] ironically referring to the moral qualities they display (but possibly a very early use of 'character' to mean 'dramatic personage').

9. *luxur*] lecher.

13. *fret*] anger, punning on 'fret' = bar used to regulate the fingering of a stringed instrument.

14. *Thou*] addressed to the skull.

15. *study's*] 'studies' (Q); the skull ornaments his study, and is what he studies.

These ragged imperfections,
When two heaven-pointed diamonds were set
In those unsightly rings—then 'twas a face   20
So far beyond the artificial shine
Of any woman's bought complexion
That the uprightest man (if such there be
That sin but seven times a day) broke custom,
And made up eight with looking after her.   25
O, she was able to ha' made a usurer's son
Melt all his patrimony in a kiss,
And what his father fifty years told
To have consumed, and yet his suit been cold.
But O, accursèd palace!   30
Thee when thou wert apparelled in thy flesh
The old duke poisoned,
Because thy purer part would not consent
Unto his palsy-lust; for old men lustful
Do show like young men, angry, eager, violent,   35
Outbid like their limited performances.
O 'ware an old man hot and vicious:
Age, as in gold, in lust is covetous.
Vengeance, thou murder's quit-rent, and whereby
Thou show'st thyself tenant to Tragedy,   40
O, keep thy day, hour, minute, I beseech,
For those thou hast determined!—Hum, who e'er knew
Murder unpaid? Faith, give Revenge her due,
Sh' has kept touch hitherto. Be merry, merry,
Advance thee, O thou terror to fat folks,   45

---

20. *unsightly rings*] ugly and sightless eye-sockets.

25. *after*] upon.

28. *told*] counted.

34–6. *old . . . performances*] i.e. like angry young men, lustful old men may appear eager and violent, but their performance is limited.

37. *'ware*] beware.

38.] marked off as a 'sentence' (Latin *sententia*), a pithy saying worthy of note by the reader.

39. *quit-rent*] rent paid by tenants in lieu of services required of them; vengeance is due as the payment for murder.

42. *determined*] decided on.

44. *kept touch*] kept faith, kept in touch.

45. *thee*] the skull.

To have their costly three-piled flesh worn off
As bare as this; for banquets, ease and laughter
Can make great men, as greatness goes by clay,
But wise men little are more great than they.

Enter his brother HIPPOLITO.

Hippolito. Still sighing o'er death's vizard?
Vindice.   Brother, welcome.   50
     What comfort bring'st thou? How go things at court?
Hippolito. In silk and silver, brother; never braver.
Vindice. Puh,
     Thou play'st upon my meaning. Prithee say,
     Has that bald Madam, Opportunity,   55
     Yet thought upon's? Speak, are we happy yet?
     Thy wrongs and mine are for one scabbard fit.
Hippolito. It may prove happiness.
Vindice.   What is't may prove?
     Give me to taste.
Hippolito.   Give me your hearing then.
     You know my place at court.
Vindice.   Ay, the Duke's chamber;   60
     But 'tis a marvel thou'rt not turned out yet!
Hippolito. Faith, I have been shoved at, but 'twas still my hap
     To hold by th' Duchess' skirt—you guess at that;
     Whom such a coat keeps up can ne'er fall flat.
     But to the purpose: 65
     Last evening, predecessor unto this,
     The Duke's son warily inquired for me,
     Whose pleasure I attended. He began
     By policy to open and unhusk me

---

46. *three-piled*] bulky; the richest velvet was made of loops formed by three threads, giving a thick pile.

48. *clay*] flesh (biblical; see Genesis 2.7).

49. *more great*] wiser, spiritually superior.

50. *vizard*] mask or face.

52. *braver*] more showily.

53. *Puh*] Pooh.

55. *bald Madam*] alluding to the common emblem figure and personification, as in the proverb 'Take Occasion by the forelock, for she is bald behind.' See also l. 99 below.

56. *happy*] in luck.

69. *policy*] craft.

About the time and common rumour;   70
But I had so much wit to keep my thoughts
Up in their built houses, yet afforded him
An idle satisfaction without danger.
But the whole aim and scope of his intent
Ended in this, conjuring me in private   75
To seek some strange-digested fellow forth,
Of ill-contented nature, either disgraced
In former times, or by new grooms displaced
Since his stepmother's nuptials; such a blood,
A man that were for evil only good—   80
To give you the true word, some base-coined pander.

Vindice. I reach you, for I know his heat is such,
Were there as many concubines as ladies
He would not be contained, he must fly out.
I wonder how ill-featured, vile-proportioned   85
That one should be, if she were made for woman,
Whom at the insurrection of his lust
He would refuse for once; heart, I think none.
Next to a skull, though more unsound than one,
Each face he meets he strongly dotes upon.   90

Hippolito. Brother, y' have truly spoke him.
He knows not you, but I'll swear you know him.

Vindice. And therefore I'll put on that knave for once,
And be a right man then, a man o' th' time,
For to be honest is not to be i' th' world.   95
Brother, I'll be that strange-composèd fellow.

---

71. *wit*] intelligence.
76. *strange-digested*] oddly disposed, rebellious.
78. *grooms*] servants.
79. *blood*] man of hot spirit, a roisterer.
81. *base-coined*] base-born and debased.
82. *reach*] understand.
86. *made for*] made to be a.
88. *heart*] by God's heart (an oath).
89–90. *Next . . . upon*] i.e. his lust would stop short only at necrophily.
Vindice is still holding the skull.
91. *spoke*] described.
92. *knows . . . know*] recognizes . . . understand.
93. *put on*] disguise myself as.
94. *right*] proper, conformist.

Hippolito. And I'll prefer you, brother.
Vindice.   Go to, then;
    The small'st advantage fattens wrongèd men.
    It may point out Occasion; if I meet her,
    I'll hold her by the foretop fast enough,   100
    Or, like the French mole, heave up hair and all.
    I have a habit that will fit it quaintly.
    Here comes our mother.
Hippolito.   And sister.
Vindice.   We must coin.
    Women are apt, you know, to take false money,
    But I dare stake my soul for these two creatures,   105
    Only excuse excepted—that they'll swallow
    Because their sex is easy in belief.

                [*Enter* GRATIANA *and* CASTIZA.]

Gratiana. What news from court, son Carlo?
Hippolito.   Faith, mother,
    'Tis whispered there, the Duchess' youngest son
    Has played a rape on lord Antonio's wife.   110
Gratiana. On that religious lady!
Castiza. Royal blood! Monster, he deserves to die,
    If Italy had no more hopes but he.
Vindice. Sister, y' have sentenced most direct and true;
    The law's a woman, and would she were you.   115
    Mother, I must take leave of you.
Gratiana.   Leave? For what?

---

97. *prefer*] recommend.
99–100. *Occasion . . . foretop*] see l. 55 and n.; 'foretop' = forelock.
101. *like . . . all*] loss of hair was one effect of syphilis, the 'French disease'.
102. *habit*] costume.
quaintly] cunningly.
103. *coin*] pretend, counterfeit.
106–7.] except that they will believe a good excuse, because women are credulous.
108. *Carlo*] mentioned only here; the author's first idea for the name of Hippolito?
Faith] an interjection = in faith, in good faith.
113. *If*] even if.
115. *The law's a woman*] Justice is often depicted as a blindfolded (impartial) woman holding scales and/or a sword.

Vindice. I intend speedy travel.

Hippolito. That he does, madam.

Gratiana.   Speedy indeed!

Vindice. For since my worthy father's funeral,
    My life's unnatural to me, e'en compelled   120
    As if I lived now when I should be dead.

Gratiana. Indeed, he was a worthy gentleman,
    Had his estate been fellow to his mind.

Vindice. The Duke did much deject him.

Gratiana.   Much!

Vindice.   Too much.
    And through disgrace, oft smothered in his spirit   125
    When it would mount, surely I think he died
    Of discontent, the nobleman's consumption.

Gratiana. Most sure he did!

Vindice.   Did he? 'Lack, you know all,
    You were his midnight secretary.

Gratiana.   No.
    He was too wise to trust me with his thoughts.   130

Vindice. I'faith, then, father, thou wast wise indeed;
    Wives are but made to go to bed and feed.
    Come, mother, sister; you'll bring me onward, brother?

Hippolito. I will.

Vindice.   I'll quickly turn into another.   *Exeunt.*

[I. ii]

> *Enter the old* Duke, LUSSURIOSO *his son, the* Duchess,
> [SPURIO] *the bastard, the Duchess's two sons* AMBITIOSO
> *and* SUPERVACUO, *the third, her youngest* [Junior Brother]
> *brought out with* Officers *for the rape; two* Judges.

Duke. Duchess, it is your youngest son. We're sorry
    His violent act has e'en drawn blood of honour,

---

120. *compelled*] forced on me.

123. *been fellow to*] matched.

124. *deject*] oppress.

125–6. *through . . . mount*] i.e. being dishonoured, and often unable to vent his mounting anger.

129. *secretary*] confidante.

132.] Proverbially women could not keep secrets; another 'sentence', as at l. 38.

>   And stained our honours;
>   Thrown ink upon the forehead of our state,
>   Which envious spirits will dip their pens into   5
>   After our death, and blot us in our tombs.
>   For that which would seem treason in our lives
>   Is laughter when we're dead. Who dares now whisper
>   That dares not then speak out, and e'en proclaim
>   With loud words and broad pens our closest shame?   10

1. Judge. Your grace hath spoke like to your silver years,
>   Full of confirmèd gravity; for what is it to have
>   A flattering false insculption on a tomb,
>   And in men's hearts reproach? The bowelled corpse
>   May be cered in, but—with free tongue I speak—   15
>   *The faults of great men through their cerecloths break.*

Duke. They do. We're sorry for 't, it is our fate
>   To live in fear, and die to live in hate.
>   I leave him to your sentence—doom him, lords,
>   The fact is great—whilst I sit by and sigh.   20

Duchess. My gracious lord, I pray be merciful.
>   Although his trespass far exceed his years,
>   Think him to be your own, as I am yours;
>   Call him not son-in-law. The law, I fear,
>   Will fall too soon upon his name and him.   25
>   Temper his fault with pity!   [*She kneels.*]

Lussurioso.   Good my lord,
>   Then 'twill not taste so bitter and unpleasant
>   Upon the judges' palate, for offences
>   Gilt o'er with mercy show like fairest women,

I.ii.4.] stained the state with shame; for other uses of 'forehead' in connection with sternness, impudence or cuckoldry, see ll. 33, 108, 176 and 201 below.

9. *then*] when we are dead.

10. *closest*] most secret.

13. *insculption*] carved inscription.

14. *bowelled*] disembowelled.

15. *cered in*] embalmed and wrapped in a cerecloth or winding-sheet.

16.] another 'sentence', as at I.i.38.

18. *die . . . hate*] be hated after we have died.

20. *fact*] crime.

24. *son-in-law*] stepson.

29. *show*] look.

  Good only for their beauties which, washed off,   30
  No sin is uglier.
Ambitioso.   I beseech your grace,
  Be soft and mild; let not relentless Law
  Look with an iron forehead on our brother.
Spurio. [*Aside*] He yields small comfort yet; hope he shall
   die,—
  And if a bastard's wish might stand in force,   35
  Would all the court were turned into a corse.
Duchess. No pity yet? Must I rise fruitless then,
  A wonder in a woman? Are my knees
  Of such low metal that without respect—
1. Judge. Let the offender stand forth.   40
  'Tis the Duke's pleasure that impartial doom
  Shall take fast hold of his unclean attempt.
  A rape! Why 'tis the very core of lust,
  Double adultery!
Junior Brother. So, sir.
2. Judge.   And which was worse,
  Committed on the lord Antonio's wife,   45
  That general-honest lady. Confess, my lord,
  What moved you to 't?
Junior Brother.   Why, flesh and blood, my lord;
  What should move men unto a woman else?
Lussurioso. O, do not jest thy doom; trust not an axe
  Or sword too far. The law is a wise serpent,   50
  And quickly can beguile thee of thy life.
  Though marriage only has made thee my brother,
  I love thee so far, play not with thy death.
Junior Brother. I thank you, troth; good admonitions, faith,—
  If I'd the grace now to make use of them.   55
1. Judge. That lady's name has spread such a fair wing
  Over all Italy, that if our tongues

---

  36. *corse*] corpse (a common early form of the word).
  38. *A . . . woman*] i.e. it is strange for a woman to be denied when she
pleads on bended knee.
  39. *low*] base, worthless.
  41. *doom*] judgement.
  42. *unclean attempt*] unchaste assault.
  46. *general-honest*] completely chaste and upright.

Were sparing toward the fact, judgement itself
Would be condemned and suffer in men's thoughts.
Junior Brother. Well then, 'tis done, and it would please me
    well   60
Were it to do again. Sure she's a goddess,
For I'd no power to see her and to live;
It falls out true in this, for I must die.
Her beauty was ordained to be my scaffold,
And yet methinks I might be easier 'sessed;   65
My fault being sport, let me but die in jest.
1. Judge. This be the sentence—
Duchess. O keep 't upon your tongue, let it not slip;
  Death too soon steals out of a lawyer's lip.
  Be not so cruel-wise!
1. Judge.   Your grace must pardon us,   70
  'Tis but the justice of the law.
Duchess.   The law
  Is grown more subtle than a woman should be.
Spurio. [*Aside*] Now, now he dies; rid 'em away!
Duchess. O what it is to have an old-cool Duke
  To be as slack in tongue as in performance.   75
1. Judge. Confirmed, this be the doom irrevocable—
Duchess. O!
1. Judge. Tomorrow early—
Duchess.   Pray be abed, my lord.
1 Judge. Your grace much wrongs yourself.
Ambitioso.   No, 'tis that tongue,
  Your too much right, does do us too much wrong.   80
1. Judge. Let that offender—
Duchess.   Live, and be in health.

---

58. *fact*] crime, as at l. 20.

62. *to live*] wishing rather to 'die' in the consummation of sexual inter-
course with her.

65. *'sessed*] assessed, judged, quibbling on 'ceased' ('ceast', Q), or brought
to rest.

71–2. *The law . . . woman*] see I.i.115 and n.

75. *performance*] i.e. in bed (as at I.i.36).

79. *wrongs*] dishonours.

80. *too much right*] too rigorous condemnation.

1. Judge. Be on a scaffold—
Duke.   Hold, hold, my lord.
Spurio. [*Aside*]   Pox on 't,
What makes my dad speak now?
Duke. We will defer the judgement till next sitting.
In the meantime let him be kept close prisoner;   85
Guard, bear him hence.
Ambitioso. [*Aside to Junior Brother*]   Brother, this makes for
thee;
Fear not, we'll have a trick to set thee free.
Junior Brother. [*Aside*] Brother, I will expect it from you both,
And in that hope I rest.
Supervacuo.   Farewell; be merry.
                              Exit [Junior Brother] *with a guard.*
Spurio. [*Aside*] Delayed, deferred—nay then, if judgement
have   90
Cold blood, flattery and bribes will kill it.
Duke. About it then, my lords, with your best powers;
More serious business calls upon our hours.
                              Exeunt [*all but the*] Duchess.
Duchess. Was 't ever known step-duchess was so mild
And calm as I? Some now would plot his death   95
With easy doctors, those loose-living men,
And make his withered grace fall to his grave
And keep church better.
Some second wife would do this, and dispatch
Her double-loathèd lord at meat or sleep.   100
Indeed, 'tis true, an old man's twice a child.
Mine cannot speak; one of his single words
Would quite have freed my youngest, dearest son

---

82. *Pox*] syphilis, invoked as a curse.
86. *makes for*] favours, helps.
92. *powers*] abilities.
95. *his*] the Duke's.
98. *keep church better*] i.e. being buried there; the 'doctors' may be of medicine or divinity.
99. *Some second wife*] some other second wife of the Duke (but not myself).
100. *or*] 'and' (Q) is probably a printer's error, caught from the line above.
101. *an . . . child*] a common proverb.

From death or durance, and have made him walk
With a bold foot upon the thorny law,   105
Whose prickles should bow under him; but 'tis not,
And therefore wedlock faith shall be forgot.
I'll kill him in his forehead, hate there feed;
That wound is deepest, though it never bleed.

[*Enter* SPURIO *at a distance.*]

And here comes he whom my heart points unto: 110
His bastard son, but my love's true-begot.
Many a wealthy letter have I sent him
Swelled up with jewels, and the timorous man
Is yet but coldly kind.
That jewel's mine that quivers in his ear,   115
Mocking his master's chillness and vain fear.
'Has spied me now.
Spurio.   Madam, your grace so private?
My duty on your hand.
Duchess. Upon my hand, sir! Troth, I think you'd fear
To kiss my hand too, if my lip stood there.   120
Spurio. Witness I would not, madam.   [*Kisses her.*]
Duchess.   'Tis a wonder,
For ceremony has made many fools;
It is as easy way unto a duchess
As to a hatted dame (if her love answer),
But that by timorous honours, pale respects,   125
Idle degrees of fear, men make their ways
Hard of themselves—what, have you thought of me?
Spurio. Madam, I ever think of you in duty,

---

104. *durance*] imprisonment.
106. *'tis not*] it is not to be.
108. *kill . . . forehead*] by cuckolding him; see l. 4 and n. above.
hate there feed] let my hate feed there.
116. *his*] its.
117. *'Has*] he has.
118. *My duty*] my dutiful kiss.
123-7. *It is . . . themselves*] men might as easily seduce a duchess as a woman of a lower class if they were not so fearful of difference in rank; men make it hard for themselves.
124. *hatted dame*] lower-class women wore hats; ladies had head-dresses.
126. *Idle*] groundless.

Regard, and—
Duchess. Puh, upon my love, I mean.
Spurio.   I would   130
    'Twere love, but 'tis a fouler name than lust.
    You are my father's wife; your grace may guess now
    What I could call it.
Duchess.   Why, th'art his son but falsely;
    'Tis a hard question whether he begot thee.
Spurio. I'faith, 'tis true too; I'm an uncertain man, of more   135
    uncertain woman. Maybe his groom o' th' stable begot
    me, you know I know not; he could ride a horse well, a
    shrewd suspicion, marry; he was wondrous tall, he had
    his length, i'faith, for peeping over half-shut holiday win-
    dows; men would desire him 'light. When he was afoot he   140
    made a goodly show under a penthouse, and when he rid
    his hat would check the signs, and clatter barbers' basins.
Duchess. Nay, set you a-horseback once, you'll ne'er 'light off.
Spurio. Indeed, I am a beggar.
Duchess. That's more the sign th' art great—but to our love.   145
    Let it stand firm both in thy thought and mind
    That the Duke was thy father, as no doubt then
    He bid fair for 't: thy injury is the more,
    For had he cut thee a right diamond,
    Thou hadst been next set in the dukedom's ring,   150
    When his worn self, like age's easy slave,
    Had dropped out of the collet into th' grave.
    What wrong can equal this? Canst thou be tame
    And think upon 't?
Spurio.   No, mad and think upon 't.

---

133. *What I would call it*] i.e. incest.

138. *marry*] an oath; originally 'by the Virgin Mary'.

140. *'light*] alight; on horseback he was tall enough to see what people were doing in private. Spurio makes out his putative father to be big and bold.

141. *penthouse*] awning over a shop or stall.
rid] rode.

142. *check the signs*] strike the shop-signs hung out over the street.

143. *basins*] shaving dishes hung out as barbers' shop-signs.

143–4. *set . . . beggar*] proverbial: 'Set a beggar on horseback, and he will never alight.'

152. *collet*] socket, or setting for a jewel. The image suggests sexual inadequacy; compare the play on 'hard' and 'stand firm', ll. 134, 146.

Duchess. Who would not be revenged of such a father,   155
    E'en in the worst way? I would thank that sin
    That could most injury him, and be in league with it.
    O what a grief 'tis, that a man should live
    But once i' th' world, and then to live a bastard,
    The curse o' the womb, the thief of nature,   160
    Begot against the seventh commandment,
    Half-damned in the conception by the justice
    Of that unbribèd everlasting law.
Spurio. O, I'd a hot-backed devil to my father.
Duchess. Would not this mad e'en patience, make blood
        rough?   165
    Who but an eunuch would not sin, his bed
    By one false minute disinherited?
Spurio. [*Aside*] Aye, there's the vengeance that my birth was
        wrapped in.
    I'll be revenged for all; now hate begin;
    I'll call foul incest but a venial sin.   170
Duchess. Cold still? In vain then must a duchess woo?
Spurio. Madam, I blush to say what I will do.
Duchess. Thence flew sweet comfort. [*She kisses him.*]
    Earnest, and farewell.
Spurio. [*Aside*] O, one incestuous kiss picks open hell.
Duchess. Faith now, old Duke, my vengeance shall reach
        high;   175
    I'll arm thy brow with woman's heraldry.   *Exit.*
Spurio. Duke, thou didst do me wrong, and by thy act
    Adultery is my nature.
    Faith, if the truth were known, I was begot
    After some gluttonous dinner; some stirring dish   180
    Was my first father, when deep healths went round

---

155. *of*] on.
157. *injury*] injure; a common early form of the verb.
161. *seventh commandment*] Exodus, 20.14, forbidding adultery.
163. *unbribèd*] uncorrupted.
165. *mad e'en patience*] make mad the most patient individual.
make blood rough] stir the blood (i.e. temper) to anger.
173. *Thence*] i.e. from your words.
Earnest] pledge of more to come.
176. *heraldry*] i.e. cuckold's horns (compare l. 108).
180. *stirring*] stimulating (as at II.1.200).

And ladies' cheeks were painted red with wine,
Their tongues as short and nimble as their heels,
Uttering words sweet and thick; and when they rose,
Were merrily disposed to fall again,—   185
In such a whisp'ring and withdrawing hour,
When base male-bawds kept sentinel at stair-head,
Was I stol'n softly; O, damnation met
The sin of feasts, drunken adultery.
I feel it swell me; my revenge is just;   190
I was begot in impudent wine and lust.
Step-mother, I consent to thy desires;
I love thy mischief well, but I hate thee,
And those three cubs thy sons, wishing confusion,
Death and disgrace may be their epitaphs.   195
As for my brother, the Duke's only son,
Whose birth is more beholding to report
Than mine, and yet perhaps as falsely sown
(Women must not be trusted with their own),
I'll loose my days upon him, hate all I;   200
Duke, on thy brow I'll draw my bastardy.
For indeed a bastard by nature should make cuckolds,
because he is the son of a cuckold-maker.   *Exit.*

[I. iii]

> *Enter* VINDICE *and* HIPPOLITO, *Vindice in disguise*
> *to attend Lord Lussurioso, the Duke's son.*

Vindice. What, brother? Am I far enough from myself?
Hippolito. As if another man had been sent whole
     Into the world, and none wist how he came.

---

183. *short*] brisk or brief in speech.
185. *fall again*] i.e. lie with any man.
188. *stol'n*] engendered by stealth.
194. *confusion*] ruin.
196. *only son*] Lussurioso, his only legitimate son.
197. *beholding to report*] beholden to reputation.
200. *loose . . . him*] i.e. spend my time persecuting him.
201. *brow*] see l. 176 and n.

I.iii.1. *far . . . myself*] well enough disguised.
3. *wist*] knew.

Vindice. It will confirm me bold, the child o' th' court.
    Let blushes dwell i' th' country. Impudence,   5
    Thou goddess of the palace, mistress of mistresses,
    To whom the costly-perfumed people pray,
    Strike thou my forehead into dauntless marble,
    Mine eyes to steady sapphires; turn my visage,
    And if I must needs glow, let me blush inward,   10
    That this immodest season may not spy
    That scholar in my cheeks, fool-bashfulness,
    That maid in the old time, whose flush of grace
    Would never suffer her to get good clothes.
    Our maids are wiser, and are less ashamed;   15
    Save Grace the bawd, I seldom hear grace named!
Hippolito. Nay, brother,
    You reach out o' th' verge now—'sfoot, the Duke's son;
    Settle your looks.
Vindice.   Pray let me not be doubted.

           [*Enter* LUSSURIOSO.]

Hippolito. My Lord—
Lussurioso.   Hippolito? [*To Vindice*] Be absent; leave us.   20
               [*Vindice withdraws to one side.*]
Hippolito. My lord, after long search, wary inquiries
    And politic siftings, I made choice of yon fellow,
    Whom I guess rare for many deep employments;
    This our age swims within him, and if time
    Had so much hair, I should take him for Time,   25
    He is so near kin to this present minute.
Lussurioso. 'Tis enough.
    We thank thee; yet words are but great men's blanks.

13–14. *That maid . . . clothes*] that old-fashioned maid who was too modest
to dress in fine clothes.

16. *grace*] i.e. grace as divine influence or virtue.

18. *reach . . . verge*] go too far.
'sfoot] by God's foot (an oath).

19. *doubted*] suspected.

22. *politic siftings*] cunning close questionings.

23. *rare*] excellent.

24. *This . . . within him*] i.e. he is a creature of our crafty times.

24–5. *if . . . hair*] Time as akin to Occasion, and proverbially bald; see
I.i.55 and 99.

28. *blanks*] worthless lottery tickets, or coins not yet stamped with a value.

Gold, though it be dumb, does utter the best thanks.

[*Gives Hippolito money.*]

Hippolito. Your plenteous honour!—An excellent fellow, my
  lord.   30

Lussurioso. So, give us leave. [*Exit* HIPPOLITO. *Vindice comes
  forward.*] Welcome; be not far off, we must be better
  acquainted. Push, be bold with us; thy hand.

Vindice. With all my heart, i'faith; how dost, sweet musk-cat?
  When shall we lie together?

Lussurioso. [*Aside*]   Wondrous knave!   35
  Gather him into boldness?—'Sfoot, the slave's
  Already as familiar as an ague,
  And shakes me at his pleasure. [*To Vindice*] Friend, I can
  Forget myself in private, but elsewhere
  I pray do you remember me.   40

Vindice. O, very well, sir—I conster myself saucy.

Lussurioso. What hast been, of what profession?

Vindice. A bone-setter.

Lussurioso. A bone-setter?

Vindice. A bawd, my lord; one that sets bones together.   45

Lussurioso. Notable bluntness!
  Fit, fit for me, e'en trained up to my hand.
  Thou hast been scrivener to much knavery then?

Vindice. Fool to abundance, sir; I have been witness to the
  surrenders of a thousand virgins, and not so little. I have   50
  seen patrimonies washed a-pieces, fruit-fields turned into

---

32. *Push*] pish; here expressing impatience, equivalent to 'come on!'

34. *musk-cat*] fop, as using perfume like musk; Vindice evidently embraces
the elegant courtier, Lussurioso.

36. *Gather . . . boldness?*] i.e. there was no need to invite him to be bold.

37. *ague*] fever.

39. *Forget myself*] i.e. forget my rank, allow you to be familiar.

40. *remember me*] show me proper respect.

41. *conster*] construe, understand.

45. *sets bones together*] i.e. brings bodies together sexually.

47. *trained . . . hand*] trained to do just what I want.

48. *scrivener to*] a notary or agent for.

49. *Fool to abundance*] in a world divided into fools and knaves (see II.ii.5),
Vindice says he has played the fool on behalf of many knaves.

50. *and not so little*] and many more women too.

51. *patrimonies . . . pieces*] i.e. estates washed away by drunkenness and
other extravagances.

51–2. *fruit-fields . . . bastards*] orchards sold to pay for the fruits of licen-
tiousness; see II.i.215–26.

bastards, and, in a world of acres, not so much dust due
to the heir 'twas left to as would well gravel a petition.
Lussurioso. [*Aside*] Fine villain! Troth, I like him wondrously;
    He's e'en shaped for my purpose. [*To Vindice*] Then
        thou know'st   55
    I' th' world strange lust?
Vindice.   O, Dutch lust, fulsome lust!
    Drunken procreation, which begets so many drunkards.
    Some father dreads not (gone to bed in wine)
    To slide from the mother and cling the daughter-in-law;
    Some uncles are adulterous with their nieces,   60
    Brothers with brothers' wives. O, hour of incest!
    Any kin now, next to the rim o' th' sister,
    Is man's meat in these days; and in the morning,
    When they are up and dressed, and their mask on,
    Who can perceive this?—save that eternal eye   65
    That sees through flesh and all. Well, if anything
    Be damned, it will be twelve o'clock at night,
    That twelve will never 'scape;
    It is the Judas of the hours, wherein
    Honest salvation is betrayed to sin.   70
Lussurioso. In troth it is, too; but let this talk glide.
    It is our blood to err, though hell gaped loud;
    Ladies know Lucifer fell, yet still are proud.
    Now, sir, wert thou as secret as thou'rt subtle,
    And deeply fathomed into all estates,   75
    I would embrace thee for a near employment,

---

53. *gravel a petition*] sprinkle sand to dry the ink on a petition to recover
lost property.

56. *Dutch lust*] or 'Drunken procreation'; the Dutch, or Germans, were
noted as heavy drinkers.

59. *cling*] i.e. in sexual embrace.

62. *rim*] (1) womb (strictly the membrane protecting it); (2) limit. See
I.i.89–90 and n.

64. *their mask on*] Women wore masks to protect their faces against
sunburn.

69. *Judas of the hours*] hour of betrayal.

71. *glide*] pass, be set aside.

75. *fathomed . . . estates*] knowledgeable about all sorts of human
conditions.

76. *near*] intimately concerning me.

And thou shouldst swell in money, and be able
To make lame beggars crouch to thee.
Vindice.   My lord,
Secret? I ne'er had that disease o' th' mother,
I praise my father. Why are men made close,   80
But to keep thoughts in best? I grant you this:
Tell but some woman a secret overnight,
Your doctor may find it in the urinal i' th' morning.
But my lord—
Lussurioso.   So; thou'rt confirmed in me,
And thus I enter thee.   [*Gives him money.*]
Vindice.   This Indian devil   85
Will quickly enter any man—but a usurer;
He prevents that, by ent'ring the devil first.
Lussurioso. Attend me; I am past my depth in lust,
And I must swim or drown. All my desires
Are levelled at a virgin not far from court,   90
To whom I have conveyed by messenger
Many waxed lines, full of my neatest spirit,
And jewels that were able to ravish her
Without the help of man; all which, and more,
She, foolish-chaste, sent back, the messengers   95
Receiving frowns for answers.
Vindice.   Possible?
'Tis a rare phoenix, whoe'er she be.
If your desires be such, she so repugnant,
In troth, my lord, I'd be revenged and marry her.
Lussurioso. Push!   100

---

79. *disease o' th' mother*] i.e. talking too much (see I.i.132); with a quibble
on 'mother' = hysteria, as at II.i.126.
80. *praise*] thank.
84. *in me*] in my trust.
85. *enter*] possess, with a hint of sexual penetration.
Indian devil] i.e. gold from the East or West Indies.
92. *waxed lines*] sealed letters.
neatest spirit] purest ardour.
93. *were*] should have been.
96. *Possible?*] is that possible?
97. *phoenix*] paragon; the mythical bird, unique in its kind, was a symbol
of excellence.
98. *repugnant*] resistant, hostile.

    The dowry of her blood, and of her fortunes,
    Are both too mean,—good enough to be bad withal.
    I am one of that number can defend
    Marriage is good, yet rather keep a friend.
    Give me my bed by stealth, there's true delight;   105
    What breeds a loathing in 't, but night by night?
Vindice. [*Aside*] A very fine religion!
Lussurioso.   Therefore thus:
    I'll trust thee in the business of my heart
    Because I see thee well experienced
    In this luxurious day wherein we breathe.   110
    Go thou, and with a smooth enchanting tongue
    Bewitch her ears, and cozen her of all grace;
    Enter upon the portion of her soul,
    Her honour, which she calls her chastity,
    And bring it into expense; for honesty   115
    Is like a stock of money laid to sleep,
    Which, ne'er so little broke, does never keep.
Vindice. You have gi'en it the tang, i'faith, my lord.
    Make known the lady to me and my brain
    Shall swell with strange invention; I will move it   120
    Till I expire with speaking, and drop down
    Without a word to save me; but I'll work—
Lussurioso. We thank thee, and will raise thee. Receive her
    name: it is the only daughter to Madam Gratiana, the
    late widow.   125

---

  101. *blood*] family.
  102. *mean*] inferior, slight.
  good . . . withal] good enough to provoke my badness, and poor enough to
make her a fit target for my lust.
  103. *can defend*] who can defend the proposition that.
  104. *friend*] lover.
  110. *luxurious*] lecherous.
  112. *cozen*] cheat.
  113. *portion*] part, but also marriage-portion or dowry.
  115. *bring . . . expense*] make her spend it, i.e. enjoy sex.
  117.] which, once it begins to be used, is quickly spent.
  118. *gi'en . . . tang*] caught its very flavour.
  120. *move*] urge.
  122. *Without . . . me*] i.e. so breathless that I won't be able to say a dying
prayer.
  123. *raise*] advance.

Vindice. [*Aside*] O, my sister, my sister!

Lussurioso. Why dost walk aside?

Vindice. My lord, I was thinking how I might begin, as thus:
    'O lady—', or twenty hundred devices her very bodkin
    will put a man in.   130

Lussurioso. Ay, or the wagging of her hair.

Vindice. No, that shall put you in, my lord.

Lussurioso. Shall't? Why, content. Dost know the daughter
    then?

Vindice. O, excellent well by sight.

Lussurioso. That was her brother that did prefer thee to us.   135

Vindice. My lord, I think so; I knew I had seen him
    somewhere—

Lussurioso. And therefore prithee let thy heart to him
    Be as a virgin, close.

Vindice.   O, my good lord.

Lussurioso. We may laugh at that simple age within him.

Vindice. Ha, ha, ha.   140

Lussurioso. Himself being made the subtle instrument
    To wind up a good fellow—

Vindice.   That's I, my lord.

Lussurioso. That's thou.
    To entice and work his sister.

Vindice.   A pure novice!

Lussurioso. 'Twas finely managed.

Vindice.   Gallantly carried.   145
    [*Aside*] A pretty perfumed villain.

Lussurioso.   I've bethought me—
    If she prove chaste still and immovable,
    Venture upon the mother, and with gifts,
    As I will furnish thee, begin with her.

Vindice. O fie, fie, that's the wrong end, my lord. 'Tis mere   150
    impossible that a mother by any gifts should become a
    bawd to her own daughter.

129–30. *bodkin . . . in*] suggest a way to begin; with a sexual suggestiveness
here and in l. 132.

139.] i.e. Hippolito is young and easily fooled.

142. *wind up*] involve, set up.

146. *perfumed*] see l. 34 above.

Lussurioso. Nay then, I see thou'rt but a puny in the subtle
　　mystery of a woman; why, 'tis held now no dainty dish.
　　The name　　　　　　　　　　　　　　　　　　　　　155
　　Is so in league with age that nowadays
　　It does eclipse three quarters of a mother.
Vindice. Does 't so, my lord?
　　Let me alone then to eclipse the fourth.
Lussurioso. Why, well said; come, I'll furnish thee, but first　160
　　Swear to be true in all.
Vindice.　　　　　　　　　True?
Lussurioso.　　　　　　　　　　　　Nay, but swear!
Vindice. Swear?
　　I hope your honour little doubts my faith.
Lussurioso. Yet for my humour's sake, 'cause I love swearing.
Vindice. 'Cause you love swearing, 'slud, I will.
Lussurioso.　　　　　　　　　　　　Why, enough.　165
　　Ere long look to be made of better stuff.
Vindice. That will do well indeed, my lord.
Lussurioso.　　　　　　　　　　　Attend me.　[*Exit.*]
Vindice. O!
　　Now let me burst; I've eaten noble poison.
　　We are made strange fellows, brother, innocent villains;　170
　　Wilt not be angry when thou hear'st on't, think'st thou?
　　I'faith, thou shalt. Swear me to foul my sister!
　　Sword, I durst make a promise of him to thee;
　　Thou shalt dis-heir him, it shall be thine honour.
　　And yet, now angry froth is down in me,　　　　　175
　　It would not prove the meanest policy
　　In this disguise to try the faith of both;
　　Another might have had the selfsame office,

---

153. *puny*] novice.
155. *name*] of bawd.
156. *age*] maturity, or possibly the present age.
165. *'slud*] = 'sblood (God's blood), a common oath.
167. *Attend me*] wait on me.
170. *fellows*] accomplices.
174. *dis-heir*] kill, and so make him cease to be the Duke's heir.
175. *down*] suppressed.
176. *the meanest policy*] the most contemptible of stratagems.
177. *both*] i.e. mother and sister.

Some slave that would have wrought effectually,
Ay, and perhaps o'erwrought 'em. Therefore I,   180
Being thought travelled, will apply myself
Unto the self same form, forget my nature,
As if no part about me were kin to 'em,
So touch 'em—though I durst almost for good
Venture my lands in heaven upon their blood.   *Exit.*   185

[I. iv]

Enter the discontented Lord ANTONIO, *whose wife the Duchess's
youngest son ravished; he discovering the body of her dead
to* [PIERO,] *certain* Lords, *and* HIPPOLITO.

Antonio. Draw nearer, lords, and be sad witnesses
Of a fair, comely building newly fall'n,
Being falsely undermined. Violent rape
Has played a glorious act; behold, my lords,
A sight that strikes man out of me.   5
Piero. That virtuous lady!
Antonio.   Precedent for wives!
Hippolito. The blush of many women, whose chaste presence
Would e'en call shame up to their cheeks and make
Pale wanton sinners have good colours.
Antonio.   Dead!
Her honour first drunk poison, and her life,   10
Being fellows in one house, did pledge her honour.
Piero. O grief of many!
Antonio.   I marked not this before—
A prayer-book the pillow to her cheek;

---

179. *slave*] villain.
180. *o'erwrought*] won over.
181. *travelled*] see I.i.117.
181-2. *apply . . . form*] adapt myself to act like the 'slave' of l. 179.
184. *touch*] test.
        for good] in the name of virtue.
185. *blood*] disposition, mettle.

I.iv.0.2. discovering] by pulling back a curtain (she may be in a bed, or
arranged like the effigy on a tomb; see ll. 13-15).
5. *strikes . . . me*] unmans me.
7-9.] i.e. her chaste presence would bring a blush of shame to the cheeks
of wanton women, whitened by the use of cosmetics.

This was her rich confection, and another
Placed in her right hand, with a leaf tucked up,   15
Pointing to these words:
Melius virtute mori, quam per dedecus vivere.
True and effectual it is indeed.
Hippolito. My lord, since you invite us to your sorrows,
    Let's truly taste 'em, that with equal comfort   20
    As to ourselves, we may relieve your wrongs;
    We have grief too, that yet walks without tongue:
    Curae leves loquuntur, maiores stupent.
Antonio. You deal with truth, my lord.
    Lend me but your attentions and I'll cut   25
    Long grief into short words. Last revelling night,
    When torch-light made an artificial noon
    About the court, some courtiers in the masque,
    Putting on better faces than their own,
    Being full of fraud and flattery—amongst whom,   30
    The Duchess' youngest son (that moth to honour)
    Filled up a room, and with long lust to eat
    Into my wearing, amongst all the ladies,
    Singled out that dear form, who ever lived
    As cold in lust as she is now in death   35
    (Which that step-duchess' monster knew too well);
    And therefore, in the height of all the revels,
    When music was heard loudest, courtiers busiest,
    And ladies great with laughter—O, vicious minute,
    Unfit but for relation to be spoke of!—   40
    Then, with a face more impudent than his vizard,

---

14. *confection*] preservative, a medical term.

17.] 'Better to die virtuous than live in dishonour'; a common saying, source unknown.

18. *effectual*] to the point.

23.] 'Small cares speak out, greater ones are struck dumb'; from Seneca's *Hippolytus*, l. 607.

28–9. *masque . . . own*] In masques courtiers were costumed and masked to represent the ideals the court was supposed to embody.

31. *moth*] as the moth destroys by eating away.

32–3. *eat . . . wearing*] like a moth destroy the clothing that belongs to me, i.e. my wife.

40. *but for relation*] if it were not essential to my narrative.

He harried her amidst a throng of panders
That live upon damnation of both kinds,
And fed the ravenous vulture of his lust
(O death to think on 't!). She, her honour forced,   45
Deemed it a nobler dowry for her name
To die with poison than to live with shame.
Hippolito. A wondrous lady, of rare fire compact;
      Sh' has made her name an empress by that act.
Piero. My lord, what judgement follows the offender?   50
Antonio. Faith, none, my lord; it cools and is deferred.
Piero. Delay the doom for rape?
Antonio.   O, you must note
      Who 'tis should die:
      The Duchess' son. She'll look to be a saver;
      Judgement in this age is near kin to favour.   55
Hippolito. Nay then, step forth, thou bribeless officer.
                                        [*Draws his sword.*]
      I bind you all in steel to bind you surely;
      Here let your oaths meet to be kept and paid,
      Which else will stick like rust, and shame the blade.
      Strengthen my vow, that if, at the next sitting,   60
      Judgement speak all in gold, and spare the blood
      Of such a serpent, e'en before their seats
      To let his soul out, which long since was found
      Guilty in heaven.
All.   We swear it, and will act it.
Antonio. Kind gentlemen, I thank you in mine ire.   65
Hippolito. 'Twere pity
      The ruins of so fair a monument
      Should not be dipped in the defacer's blood.
Piero. Her funeral shall be wealthy, for her name
      Merits a tomb of pearl. My lord Antonio,   70

---

42. *harried*] violated.
43. *damnation . . . kinds*] by sinning themselves, and corrupting others.
48. *of . . . compact*] made up of elements of the rarest quality.
49. *empress*] perhaps punning on 'impress' = emblem.
58. *Here*] where their swords meet; recalling Hamlet swearing his friends to secrecy in *Hamlet*, I.v.
60. *sitting*] session of the court.
61. *Judgement . . . gold*] i.e. justice is perverted by wealth and influence.

For this time wipe your lady from your eyes;
No doubt our grief and yours may one day court it,
When we are more familiar with revenge.
Antonio. That is my comfort, gentlemen, and I joy
    In this one happiness above the rest,   75
    Which will be called a miracle at last:
    That, being an old man, I'd a wife so chaste.   *Exeunt.*

---

72. *court it*] be shown at court.

Act II

Enter CASTIZA, *the sister.*

Castiza. How hardly shall that maiden be beset
    Whose only fortunes are her constant thoughts;
    That has no other child's-part but her honour
    That keeps her low and empty in estate.
    Maids and their honours are like poor beginners;   5
    Were not sin rich, there would be fewer sinners.
    Why had not virtue a revenue? Well,
    I know the cause, 'twould have impoverished hell.

[*Enter* DONDOLO.]

    How now, Dondolo?

Dondolo. Madonna, there is one, as they say, a thing of flesh   10
    and blood, a man I take him by his beard, that would very
    desirously mouth to mouth with you.

Castiza. What's that?

Dondolo. Show his teeth in your company.

Castiza. I understand thee not.   15

Dondolo. Why, speak with you, Madonna.

Castiza. Why, say so, madman, and cut off a great deal of
    dirty way; had it not been better spoke in ordinary words,
    that one would speak with me?

Dondolo. Ha, ha; that's as ordinary as two shillings. I would   20
    strive a little to show myself in my place; a gentleman-
    usher scorns to use the phrase and fancy of a serving-
    man.

Castiza. Yours be your own, sir. Go, direct him hither.

[*Exit* DONDOLO.]

II.i.1. *hardly . . . beset*] assailed by temptations.
3. *child's-part*] inheritance.
9. *Dondolo*] a type name for a foolish courtier.
21. *place*] office.

I hope some happy tidings from my brother   25
That lately travelled, whom my soul affects.
Here he comes.

Enter VINDICE *her brother, disguised.*

Vindice. Lady, the best of wishes to your sex,
    Fair skins and new gowns.   [*Presents her with a letter.*]
Castiza.   O, they shall thank you, sir.
    Whence this?
Vindice.   O, from a dear and worthy friend,   30
    Mighty!
Castiza.   From whom?
Vindice.   The Duke's son.
Castiza.   Receive that!
            A box o' th' ear to her brother.
    I swore I'd put anger in my hand,
    And pass the virgin limits of myself
    To him that next appeared in that base office,
    To be his sin's attorney. Bear to him   35
    That figure of my hate upon thy cheek
    Whilst 'tis yet hot, and I'll reward thee for 't;
    Tell him my honour shall have a rich name
    When several harlots shall share his with shame.
    Farewell; commend me to him in my hate!   *Exit.*   40
Vindice. It is the sweetest box that e'er my nose came nigh,
    The finest drawn-work cuff that e'er was worn!
    I'll love this blow for ever, and this cheek
    Shall still henceforward take the wall of this.
    O, I'm above my tongue! Most constant sister,   45

---

26. *affects*] loves.

29. *they*] i.e. other women, others of my sex.

30. *this*] a letter, or possibly a jewel.

33.] i.e. go beyond the limits of behaviour proper to a virgin.

35. *his*] Lussurioso's.

41. *box*] as if the box on the ear were a box of sweet-smelling ointment.

42. *drawn-work cuff*] a cuff decorated with patterned threads, but punning also on 'cuff' = blow.

44. *take the wall of this*] take precedence over my other cheek; as it was cleaner and safer to keep next to the wall in walking along a street.

45. *I'm above my tongue*] i.e. I am happier than I can say.

In this thou hast right honourable shown;
Many are called by their honour that have none.
Thou art approved for ever in my thoughts.
It is not in the power of words to taint thee;
And yet for the salvation of my oath,   50
As my resolve in that point, I will lay
Hard siege unto my mother, though I know
A siren's tongue could not bewitch her so.
Mass, fitly here she comes; thanks, my disguise.—
Madam, good afternoon.

[*Enter* GRATIANA.]

Gratiana.   Y'are welcome, sir.   55
Vindice. The next of Italy commends him to you,
   Our mighty expectation, the Duke's son.
                    [*Presents her with a letter.*]
Gratiana. I think myself much honoured that he pleases
   To rank me in his thoughts.
Vindice.   So may you, lady.
   One that is like to be our sudden duke—   60
   The crown gapes for him every tide—and then
   Commander o'er us all. Do but think on him;
   How blest were they now that could pleasure him
   E'en with anything almost.
Gratiana.   Ay, save their honour!
Vindice. Tut, one would let a little of that go too,   65
   And ne'er be seen in 't—ne'er be seen in 't, mark you;
   I'd wink, and let it go—
Gratiana.   Marry, but I would not.
Vindice. Marry, but I would, I hope; I know you would too,

---

46. *right honourable*] quibbling on the form of address proper to peers and
others of high rank.

50. *oath*] see I.iii.164–5.

51. *resolve*] to try the faith of his sister and mother; see I.iii.177.

54. *Mass*] by the Mass (an oath).

56. *next*] next ruler.

60. *like*] likely.

61. *every tide*] every hour, any minute now.

64. *save their honour*] except their chastity.

67. *wink*] close my eyes.

If you'd that blood now which you gave your daughter.
To her indeed 'tis this wheel comes about;   70
That man that must be all this, perhaps ere morning
(For his white father does but mould away),
Has long desired your daughter—
Gratiana. Desired?
Vindice.   —Nay, but hear me;
He desires now that will command hereafter.   75
Therefore be wise; I speak as more a friend
To you than him. Madam, I know y'are poor,
And, 'lack the day,
There are too many poor ladies already;
Why should you vex the number? 'Tis despised;   80
Live wealthy, rightly understand the world,
And chide away that foolish country-girl
Keeps company with your daughter, chastity.
Gratiana. O fie, fie; the riches of the world cannot hire a
mother to such a most unnatural task!   85
Vindice. No, but a thousand angels can;
Men have no power, angels must work you to 't.
The world descends into such base-born evils
That forty angels can make fourscore devils.
There will be fools still I perceive, still fools;   90
Would I be poor, dejected, scorned of greatness,
Swept from the palace, and see other daughters
Spring with the dew o' th' court, having mine own
So much desired and loved—by the Duke's son?
No, I would raise my state upon her breast,   95
And call her eyes my tenants; I would count

---

70. *wheel*] wheel of Fortune.
72. *white*] white-haired.
78. *'lack the day*] shame on (alack) the present age.
80. *vex*] trouble, by adding to it.
83. *Keeps*] who keeps.
86. *angels*] gold coins, bearing the figure of St Michael (and playing on the idea of angels in heaven).
91. *dejected*] lowly, disadvantaged.
95. *state*] status and wealth or estate.
96. *call . . . tenants*] i.e. make money from her beauty, as if her eyes were tenants paying rent.

My yearly maintenance upon her cheeks,
Take coach upon her lip, and all her parts
Should keep men after men, and I would ride
In pleasure upon pleasure.   100
You took great pains for her, once when it was;
Let her requite it now, though it be but some;
You brought her forth, she well may bring you home.
Gratiana. O heavens!
This overcomes me.
Vindice. [*Aside*]   Not, I hope, already!   105
Gratiana. [*Aside*] It is too strong for me. Men know that
      know us;
We are so weak, their words can overthrow us.
He touched me nearly, made my virtues bate,
When his tongue struck upon my poor estate.
Vindice. [*Aside*] I e'en quake to proceed; my spirit turns edge. 110
I fear me she's unmothered, yet I'll venture.
That woman is all male, whom none can enter.
[*To her*] What think you now, lady? Speak, are you wiser?
What said advancement to you? Thus it said:
The daughter's fall lifts up the mother's head.   115
Did it not, madam? But I'll swear it does.
In many places, tut, this age fears no man;
'Tis no shame to be bad, because 'tis common.
Gratiana. Ay, that's the comfort on 't.
Vindice.   The comfort on 't?
I keep the best for last; can these persuade you   120
To forget heaven—and—   [*Gives her money.*]
Gratiana. Ay, these are they—
Vindice. O!
Gratiana.   —that enchant our sex, these are

---

97. *maintenance*] means of support.
99. *men after men*] more and more servants.
101. *when it was*] i.e. at her birth.
102. *but some*] only in part.
103. *bring you home*] i.e. make you rich.
108. *bate*] weaken, abate.
110. *turns edge*] becomes blunt, is dulled.
112, 118.] Italicised as maxims or 'sentences'; see I.i.38 and n.
112. enter] win over, and sexually penetrate (compare I.iii.85).

The means that govern our affections.
That woman   125
Will not be troubled with the mother long,
That sees the comfortable shine of you;
I blush to think what for your sakes I'll do.
Vindice. [*Aside*] O suff'ring heaven, with thy invisible finger,
E'en at this instant turn the precious side   130
Of both mine eyeballs inward, not to see myself!
Gratiana. Look you, sir.
Vindice.   Holla!
Gratiana.   Let this thank your pains.
Vindice. O, you're a kind madam.
Gratiana. I'll see how I can move.
Vindice.   Your words will sting.
Gratiana. If she be still chaste, I'll ne'er call her mine.   135
Vindice. [*Aside*] Spoke truer than you mean it.
Gratiana. [*Calling*] Daughter Castiza!

[*Enter* CASTIZA.]

Castiza. Madam.
Vindice. O, she's yonder; meet her.
[*Aside*] Troops of celestial soldiers guard her heart!   140
Yon dam has devils enough to take her part.
Castiza. Madam, what makes yon evil-officed man
In presence of you?
Gratiana.   Why?
Castiza.   He lately brought
Immodest writing sent from the Duke's son
To tempt me to dishonourable act.   145
Gratiana. Dishonourable act?—Good honourable fool,
That wouldst be honest 'cause thou wouldst be so,
Producing no one reason but thy will.
And 't has a good report, prettily commended,
But pray, by whom?—mean people, ignorant people;   150

---

126. *mother*] (1) maternal affection (2) hysteria; see I.iii.79 and n.
129. *finger*] see Exodus 8.19 and Luke 12.20 for the phrase 'the finger of God'.
132. *Let . . . pains*] she tips Vindice.
134. *move*] persuade.
147. *honest*] virtuous.

The better sort I'm sure cannot abide it.
And by what rule should we square out our lives,
But by our betters' actions? O if thou knew'st
What 'twere to lose it, thou would never keep it;
But there's a cold curse laid upon all maids;   155
Whilst others clip the sun, they clasp the shades.
Virginity is paradise locked up;
You cannot come by your selves without fee,
And 'twas decreed that man should keep the key.
Deny advancement? treasure? the Duke's son?   160

Castiza. I cry you mercy, lady, I mistook you;
Pray, did you see my mother? Which way went she?
Pray God I have not lost her.

Vindice. [*Aside*]   Prettily put by.

Gratiana. Are you as proud to me as coy to him?
Do you not know me now?

Castiza.   Why, are you she?   165
The world's so changed, one shape into another,
It is wise child now that knows her mother!

Vindice. [*Aside*] Most right, i'faith.

Gratiana.   I owe your cheek my hand
For that presumption now, but I'll forget it;
Come, you shall leave those childish 'haviours,   170
And understand your time. Fortunes flow to you;
What, will you be a girl?
If all feared drowning that spy waves ashore,
Gold would grow rich, and all the merchants poor.

Castiza. It is pretty saying of a wicked one,   175
But methinks now

156.] (1) while others enjoy life and warmth, maids are left in the shade and cold (2) while others embrace the ruler (the 'sun'), maids meet death (like Vindice's betrothed, Gloriana).

158. *come by your selves*] i.e. discover or possess your 'paradise'.

163. *put by*] turned aside, evaded.

164. *coy*] disdainful.

167.] varying the proverb, 'It is a wise child that knows his own father.'

168–9. *I owe . . . now*] i.e. I ought to slap you for that insolence.

173. *ashore*] i.e. from the shore.

174.] i.e. merchants would not venture their money in trade, and gold would accumulate.

It does not show so well out of your mouth,
Better in his.
Vindice. [*Aside*]   Faith, bad enough in both,
Were I in earnest, as I'll seem no less—
[*To Castiza*] I wonder, lady, your own mother's words   180
Cannot be taken, nor stand in full force.
'Tis honesty you urge; what's honesty?
'Tis but heaven's beggar, and what woman is
So foolish to keep honesty,
And be not able to keep herself? No,   185
Times are grown wiser and will keep less charge;
A maid that has small portion now intends
To break up house, and live upon her friends.
How blest are you!—You have happiness alone;
Others must fall to thousands, you to one,   190
Sufficient in himself to make your forehead
Dazzle the world with jewels, and petitionary people
Start at your presence.
Gratiana.   O, if I were young,
I should be ravished.
Castiza.   Ay, to lose your honour.
Vindice. 'Slid, how can you lose your honour to deal with my   195
lord's grace?
He'll add more honour to it by his title;
Your mother will tell you how.
Gratiana.   That I will.
Vindice. O, think upon the pleasure of the palace;
Securèd ease and state; the stirring meats   200
Ready to move out of the dishes that
E'en now quicken when they're eaten;
Banquets abroad by torch-light, music, sports,
Bare-headed vassals that had ne'er the fortune

---

186. *keep less charge*] (1) maintain less expense (2) take less care (about virtue).
187. *intends*] resolves.
191. *forehead*] see I.ii.4 and n.
192. *petitionary*] petitioning at court.
195. *'Slid*] by His (God's) eyelid (an oath).
200. *stirring*] stimulating.
202. *quicken*] excite, quibbling on the sense 'make pregnant'.

To keep on their own hats, but let horns wear 'em;   205
Nine coaches waiting,—hurry, hurry, hurry!

Castiza. Ay, to the devil.

Vindice. [*Aside*] Ay, to the devil—[*To her*] To th' Duke, by
    my faith.

Gratiana. Ay, to the Duke. Daughter, you'd scorn to think o'
    th' devil an you were there once.   210

Vindice. [*Aside*] True, for most there are as proud as he for his
    heart, i'faith.—

    [*To Castiza*] Who'd sit at home in a neglected room,
Dealing her short-lived beauty to the pictures
That are as useless as old men, when those   215
Poorer in face and fortune than herself
Walk with a hundred acres on their backs,
Fair meadows cut into green foreparts—O,
It was the greatest blessing ever happened to women,
When farmers' sons agreed, and met again,   220
To wash their hands and come up gentlemen;
The commonwealth has flourished ever since.
Lands that were mete by the rod, that labour's spared,
Tailors ride down and measure 'em by the yard;
Fair trees, those comely foretops of the field,   225
Are cut to maintain head-tires—much untold;
All thrives but chastity, she lies a-cold.
Nay, shall I come nearer to you? Mark but this:
why are there so few honest women, but because 'tis the
poorer profession? That's accounted best that's best   230
followed; least in trade, least in fashion; and that's

205.] Men of lower rank removed their hats in the presence of the Duke;
'horns' hints at cuckoldry by their social superiors.

210. *an*] if.

214.] i.e. sharing her beauty with the paintings on the walls.

217–26. *Walk . . . head-tires*] These ironic lines reflect a common satirical
complaint of the age, marking a drift from the country (typifying honesty) to
the court (symbol of corruption), land being sold to provide money for
expensive clothes and display.

218. *foreparts*] stomachers, coverings for the breast.

223. *mete . . . rod*] measured by the statutory unit of 5.5 yards.

224. *yard*] tailor's or cloth-yard.

225. *foretops*] properly, forelocks, as at I.i.100.

226. *head-tires*] head-dresses.

not honesty, believe it; and do but note the low and
dejected price of it:
Lose but a pearl, we search and cannot brook it,
But that once gone, who is so mad to look it?   235
Gratiana. Troth, he says true.
Castiza.   False, I defy you both.
   I have endured you with an ear of fire;
   Your tongues have struck hot irons on my face.
   Mother, come from that poisonous woman there!
Gratiana. Where?   240
Castiza. Do you not see her? She's too inward, then.
   [*To Vindice*] Slave, perish in thy office.—You heavens,
      please
   Henceforth to make the mother a disease,
   Which first begins with me; yet I've outgone you.   *Exit.*
Vindice. [*Aside*] O angels, clap your wings upon the skies,   245
   And give this virgin crystal plaudities!
Gratiana. Peevish, coy, foolish!—But return this answer:
   My lord shall be most welcome when his pleasure
   Conducts him this way. I will sway mine own;
   Women with women can work best alone.   *Exit.*   250
Vindice. Indeed, I'll tell him so.
   O, more uncivil, more unnatural

---

234. brook it] put up with its loss.

235. that] i.e. chastity.

   look it] be concerned about it.

237. *with an ear of fire*] i.e. with ears reddened and burning with shame.

241. *She's too inward*] i.e. the invisible 'poisonous woman' is too much a
part of her inner being, and Gratiana cannot recognise her own corruption.

242. *Slave*] villain, as at I.iii.179.

243-4. *make . . . outgone you*] Castiza seems to say that she is the first to
suffer 'the mother' in the sense of hysteria, but that she has gone beyond the
two of them in escaping the disease common to many mothers (see l. 126 and
n.) of exploiting their daughters' chastity.

244. *outgone you*] perhaps = circumvented, if 'you' refers to Gratiana and
Vindice, but the exact sense is not clear.

246. *crystal plaudities*] clear applause; 'crystal' refers to the crystalline
sphere of Ptolemaic astronomy, supposed to revolve between heaven and
earth.

247. *Peevish*] headstrong.

249. *sway mine own*] i.e. control the behaviour of my daughter.

252. *uncivil*] barbarous.

Than those base-titled creatures that look downward!
Why does not heaven turn black, or with a frown
Undo the world?—Why does not earth start up,   255
And strike the sins that tread upon 't? O,
were 't not for gold and women, there would be no
damnation; hell would look like a lord's great kitchen
without fire in 't.
But 'twas decreed before the world began,   260
That they should be the hooks to catch at man.   *Exit.*

[II. ii]

      Enter LUSSURIOSO, *with* HIPPOLITO, *Vindice's brother.*

Lussurioso. I much applaud
    Thy judgement; thou art well-read in a fellow,
    And 'tis the deepest art to study man.
    I know this, which I never learned in schools:
    The world's divided into knaves and fools.   5
Hippolito. [*Aside*] 'Knave' in your face, my lord—behind
    your back.
Lussurioso. And I much thank thee that thou hast preferred
    A fellow of discourse, well mingled,
    And whose brain time hath seasoned.
Hippolito.   True, my lord.
    [*Aside*] We shall find season once, I hope. O villain,   10
    To make such an unnatural slave of me—but—
Lussurioso. Mass, here he comes.

        [*Enter* VINDICE *disguised.*]

Hippolito. [*Aside to Vindice*] And now shall I have free leave
    to depart.
Lussurioso. Your absence; leave us.
Hippolito. [*Aside to Vindice*]   Are not my thoughts true?
    I must remove, but brother, you may stay;   15

253.] referring probably to animals in general, with a suggestion of beastliness.

II.ii.8. *discourse*] skilled conversation.
10. *find season*] i.e. find a time to deal with Lussurioso.
15–16.] Hippolito speaks about his brother, but addresses the audience.

Heart, we are both made bawds a new-found way!

Exit.

Lussurioso.　Now,
We're an even number; a third man's dangerous,
Especially her brother. Say, be free,
Have I a pleasure toward?

Vindice.　　　　　　　　O, my lord.　　　　　20

Lussurioso.　Ravish me in thine answer; art thou rare?
Hast thou beguiled her of salvation,
And rubbed hell o'er with honey? Is she a woman?

Vindice.　In all but in desire.

Lussurioso.　　　　　　　Then she's in nothing—
I bate in courage now.

Vindice.　　　　　　　The words I brought　　　25
Might well have made indifferent-honest naught;
A right good woman in these days is changed
Into white money with less labour far.
Many a maid has turned to Mahomet
With easier working; I durst undertake,　　　30
Upon the pawn and forfeit of my life,
With half those words to flat a puritan's wife.
But she is close and good—yet 'tis a doubt
By this time. O, the mother, the mother!

Lussurioso.　I never thought their sex had been a wonder　　35
Until this minute. What fruit from the mother?

Vindice.　[*Aside*] Now must I blister my soul, be forsworn,
Or shame the woman that received me first.
I will be true, thou liv'st not to proclaim;
Spoke to a dying man, shame has no shame.—　　40

---

20. *toward*] in prospect.

21. *rare*] successful; compare I.iii.23.

25. *bate in courage*] i.e. lose something of my desire for her, or eagerness to seduce her.

brought] took to her.

26. *indifferent-honest naught*] someone of ordinary virtue wicked.

28. *white money*] silver coin (in prostitution).

29. *has . . . Mahomet*] i.e. has turned pagan (and abandoned Christian morality).

32. *flat*] overthrow.

38. *received me first*] i.e. greeted me at my birth.

39. *thou*] Lussurioso.

[*To him*] My lord!

Lussurioso.   Who's that?

Vindice.   Here's none but I, my lord.

Lussurioso. What would thy haste utter?

Vindice.   Comfort.

Lussurioso.   Welcome.

Vindice. The maid being dull, having no mind to travel
    Into unknown lands, what did me I straight
    But set spurs to the mother; golden spurs   45
    Will put her to a false gallop in a trice.

Lussurioso. Is 't possible that in this
    The mother should be damned before the daughter?

Vindice. O, that's good manners, my lord; the mother for her
    age must go foremost, you know.   50

Lussurioso. Thou'st spoke that true; but where comes in this
    comfort?

Vindice. In a fine place, my lord—the unnatural mother
    Did with her tongue so hard beset her honour
    That the poor fool was struck to silent wonder;
    Yet still the maid, like an unlighted taper,   55
    Was cold and chaste, save that her mother's breath
    Did blow fire on her cheeks. The girl departed,
    But the good ancient madam, half mad, threw me
    These promising words, which I took deeply note of:
    'My lord shall be most welcome—'

Lussurioso.   Faith, I thank her.   60

Vindice. 'When his pleasure conducts him this way—'

Lussurioso. That shall be soon, i'faith.

Vindice.   'I will sway mine own—'

Lussurioso. She does the wiser; I commend her for 't.

Vindice. 'Women with women can work best alone.'

Lussurioso. By this light, and so they can; give 'em their due,   65
    men are not comparable to 'em.

Vindice. No, that's true, for you shall have one woman knit
    more in an hour than any man can ravel again in seven
    and twenty year.

---

44. *did me I straight*] did I do straightway.
65. *By this light*] a common oath, = by God's light, the light of day.
68. *ravel*] unravel.

Lussurioso. Now my desires are happy; I'll make 'em freemen
  now.   70
  Thou art a precious fellow; faith, I love thee.
  Be wise, and make it thy revenue: beg, leg;
  What office couldst thou be ambitious for?
Vindice. Office, my lord? Marry, if I might have my wish, I
  would have one that was never begged yet.   75
Lussurioso. Nay, then, thou canst have none.
Vindice. Yes, my lord, I could pick out another office yet, nay,
  and keep a horse and drab upon 't.
Lussurioso. Prithee, good bluntness, tell me.
Vindice. Why, I would desire but this, my lord: to have all the 80
  fees behind the arras, and all the farthingales that fall
  plump about twelve o'clock at night upon the rushes.
Lussurioso. Thou'rt a mad apprehensive knave. Dost think to
  make any great purchase of that?
Vindice. O, 'tis an unknown thing, my lord; I wonder 't has 85
  been missed so long!
Lussurioso. Well, this night I'll visit her, and 'tis till then
  A year in my desires; farewell. Attend;
  Trust me with thy preferment.   *Exit.*
Vindice.   My loved lord.
  [*Drawing his sword*] O, shall I kill him o' th' wrong side
   now? No!   90
  Sword, thou wast never a back-biter yet.
  I'll pierce him to his face;

---

70. *I'll . . . freemen*] i.e. I'll give my desires free rein.

72. *beg, leg*] beg by making a leg.

76.] i.e. all official positions at court are begged in return for services.
Lussurioso in effect says that the whole system is corrupt.

78. *drab*] mistress.

81. *fees . . . arras*] fees for assignations in the space between wall-hangings
and the wall. (Vindice implies that if he had these fees he would soon be
rich.)

farthingales] hooped petticoats.

82. *plump*] smack, in haste.

rushes] commonly strewn on floors (and theatre stages).

83. *apprehensive*] sharp-witted.

84. *purchase*] profit.

85. *unknown*] unnoticed.

90. *o' th' wrong side*] i.e. by stabbing him in the back.

He shall die looking upon me.
Thy veins are swelled with lust, this shall unfill 'em;
Great men were gods, if beggars could not kill 'em.   95
Forgive me, heaven, to call my mother wicked!
O, lessen not my days upon the earth.
I cannot honour her; by this I fear me
Her tongue has turned my sister into use.
I was a villain not to be forsworn   100
To this our lecherous hope, the Duke's son;
For lawyers, merchants, some divines, and all
Count beneficial perjury a sin small.
It shall go hard yet, but I'll guard her honour,
And keep the ports sure.   105

Enter HIPPOLITO.

Hippolito. Brother, how goes the world? I would know news
Of you, but I have news to tell you.
Vindice.   What,
In the name of knavery?
Hippolito.   Knavery, faith;
This vicious old Duke's worthily abused;
The pen of his bastard writes him cuckold.   110
Vindice. His bastard?
Hippolito.   Pray believe it; he and the Duchess
By night meet in their linen. They have been seen
By stair-foot panders.
Vindice.   O, sin foul and deep!
Great faults are winked at when the Duke's asleep.
See, see, here comes the Spurio.
Hippolito.   Monstrous luxur!   115

[*Enter* SPURIO *with two* Servants. *Vindice
and Hippolito stand aside.*]

---

97. *lessen . . . earth*] recalling Exodus 20.12, 'Honour thy father and thy
mother, that thy days may be prolonged . . .' (Geneva Bible).
99. *use*] employment for sexual purposes, and profit; see IV.iv.103 and n.
103. *beneficial*] i.e. for a good cause.
105. *ports*] gates (of chastity).
110. *pen*] suggesting 'penis'.
115. *luxur*] lecher, as at I.i.9.

Vindice. Unbraced; two of his valiant bawds with him.
    O, there's a wicked whisper; hell is in his ear.
    Stay, let's observe his passage.—
Spurio.   O, but are you sure on 't?
I. Servant. My lord, most sure on 't, for 'twas spoke by one
    That is most inward with the Duke's son's lust: 120
    That he intends within this hour to steal
    Unto Hippolito's sister, whose chaste life
    The mother has corrupted for his use.
Spurio. Sweet word, sweet occasion! Faith, then, brother,
    I'll disinherit you in as short time   125
    As I was when I was begot in haste;
    I'll damn you at your pleasure—precious deed!
    After your lust, O, 'twill be fine to bleed.
    Come, let our passing out be soft and wary.
                      Exeunt [SPURIO *and* Servants].
Vindice. Mark, there, there, that step; now to the Duchess.   130
    This, their second meeting, writes the Duke cuckold
    With new additions, his horns newly revived.
    Night, thou that look'st like funeral heralds' fees
    Torn down betimes i' th' morning; thou hang'st fitly
    To grace those sins that have no grace at all.   135
    Now 'tis full sea abed over the world;
    There's juggling of all sides. Some that were maids
    E'en at sunset are now perhaps i' th' toll-book.
    This woman in immodest thin apparel
    Lets in her friend by water; here a dame,   140

---

116. *Unbraced*] with clothes unfastened.

118. *observe*] Vindice and Hippolito watch unseen, and do not hear the dialogue between Spurio and the servant.

120. *is most inward with*] has an intimate knowledge of.

124. *brother*] i.e. the absent Lussurioso.

133. *funeral heralds' fees*] i.e. the money heralds made by charging for displays of escutcheons, pennons, etc., advertising at funerals the prized gentility of the dead person.

134. *betimes*] early.

136. *full sea*] high tide (in sexual activity).

137. *juggling of*] deception on.

138. *toll-book*] literally, the register of animals for sale at a market.

139. *This woman*] i.e. one woman, for instance.

140. *by water*] suggesting the Thames? or Venetian canals?

Cunning, nails leather hinges to a door
To avoid proclamation; now cuckolds are
A-coining, apace, apace, apace, apace;
And careful sisters spin that thread i' th' night
That does maintain them and their bawds i' th' day.   145
Hippolito. You flow well, brother.
Vindice.   Puh, I'm shallow yet,
Too sparing and too modest—shall I tell thee?
If every trick were told that's dealt by night,
There are few here that would not blush outright.
Hippolito. I am of that belief too.
Vindice.   Who's this comes?   150

[*Enter* LUSSURIOSO.]

The Duke's son up so late?—Brother, fall back,
And you shall learn some mischief. [*Hippolito retires.*]—
      My good lord.
Lussurioso. Piato! Why, the man I wished for. Come,
      I do embrace this season for the fittest
      To taste of that young lady.
Vindice. [*Aside*]   Heart and hell!   155
Hippolito. [*Aside*] Damned villain!
Vindice. [*Aside*] I ha' no way now to cross it, but to kill him.
Lussurioso. Come; only thou and I.
Vindice.   My lord, my lord!
Lussurioso. Why dost thou start us?
Vindice.   I'd almost forgot—
      The bastard!
Lussurioso.   What of him?
Vindice.   This night, this hour—   160
      This minute, now—
Lussurioso.   What, what?
Vindice.   Shadows the Duchess—

---

141. *leather hinges*] i.e. as more silent than metal ones.
143. *A-coining*] being minted, produced in quantity.
144. *sisters*] prostitutes.
spin that thread] like silkworms, using their bodies.
149. *here*] in the audience, as well as at court.
153. *Piato*] meaning 'hidden'; the first mention of Vindice's assumed name.
157. *cross*] thwart.
159. *start us*] startle me (royal plural).
161. *Shadows*] covers.

Lussurioso. Horrible word!
Vindice.   And like strong poison eats
   Into the Duke your father's forehead.
Lussurioso.   O!
Vindice. He makes horn-royal.
Lussurioso.   Most ignoble slave!
Vindice. This is the fruit of two beds.
Lussurioso.   I am mad.   165
Vindice. That passage he trod warily.
Lussurioso.   He did?
Vindice. And hushed his villains every step he took.
Lussurioso. His villains? I'll confound them.
Vindice. Take 'em finely, finely now.
Lussurioso. The Duchess' chamber-door shall not control
      me.   170

                    Exeunt [LUSSURIOSO *and* VINDICE].

Hippolito. Good, happy, swift; there's gunpowder i' th' court,
      Wild-fire at midnight. In this heedless fury
      He may show violence to cross himself;
      I'll follow the event.   *Exit.*

[II. iii]

      Enter again [LUSSURIOSO, *with drawn sword, and* VINDICE;
         the Duke *and* Duchess *screened within a bed*].

Lussurioso. Where is that villain?
Vindice. Softly, my lord, and you may take 'em twisted.
Lussurioso. I care not how.
Vindice.   O, 'twill be glorious

162-3. *eats . . . forehead*] in shame, and as cuckolding him; see I.ii.4.
164. *makes horn-royal*] cuckolds the Duke.
165. *fruit . . . beds*] i.e. lechery, or lying in other beds than one's own.
166. *That passage*] Vindice indicates the route Spurio took at l. 129.
167. *villains*] accomplices.
169. *finely*] cunningly.
172. *Wild-fire*] inflammable material (used to start fires in warfare).
173. *show . . . himself*] thwart his purpose by the violence he shows.
174. *event*] outcome.

II.iii.0.1-2.] A property four-poster bed, curtained, as was usual, has to be
thrust out or revealed at this point; Lussurioso pulls back the curtain at l. 8.
   2. *twisted*] coupling.

To kill 'em doubled, when they're heaped. Be soft,
My lord.

Lussurioso.   Away, my spleen is not so lazy;   5
Thus, and thus, I'll shake their eyelids ope,
And with my sword shut 'em again for ever.
Villain! Strumpet!

[*He reveals the Duke and Duchess in bed.*]

Duke. You upper guard defend us—
Duchess. Treason, treason!
Duke.   —O, take me not   10
In sleep! I have great sins, I must have days,
Nay, months, dear son, with penitential heaves,
To lift 'em out, and not to die unclear.
O, thou wilt kill me both in heaven and here.
Lussurioso. I am amazed to death.
Duke.   Nay, villain, traitor,   15
Worse than the foulest epithet, now I'll gripe thee
E'en with the nerves of wrath, and throw thy head
Amongst the lawyers. Guard!

[*The* Guard *enters and seizes Lussurioso.*]
Enter [HIPPOLITO,] Nobles, *and* [AMBITIOSO *and*
SUPERVACUO, *the Duchess's*] *sons.*

1. Noble. How comes the quiet of your grace disturbed?
Duke. This boy, that should be myself after me,   20
Would be myself before me; and in heat
Of that ambition bloodily rushed in,
Intending to depose me in my bed.
2. Noble. Duty and natural loyalty forfend!
Duchess. He called his father villain, and me strumpet,   25
A word that I abhor to file my lips with.
Ambitioso. That was not so well done, brother.
Lussurioso.   I am abused—

---

5. *spleen*] anger.
9. *upper*] nearest the bedchamber.
12. *heaves*] sighs.
13. *unclear*] in sin.
17. *nerves*] sinews.
26. *file*] defile.
27. *abused*] deceived, imposed upon.

I know there's no excuse can do me good.

Vindice. [*Aside to Hippolito*] 'Tis now good policy to be from
    sight;
  His vicious purpose to our sister's honour   30
  Is crossed beyond our thought.

Hippolito. [*Aside to Vindice*]   You little dreamt
  His father slept here.

Vindice. [*Aside to Hippolito*] O, 'twas far beyond me—
  But since it fell so, without frightful words,
  Would he had killed him; 'twould have eased our swords!

        [VINDICE *and* HIPPOLITO] *dissemble a flight*
                [*and steal away*].

Duke. Be comforted, our Duchess, he shall die.   35

                [*Exit* Duchess.]

Lussurioso. Where's this slave-pander now? Out of mine eye,
  Guilty of this abuse!

      Enter SPURIO *with* [*two* Servants,] *his villains.*

Spurio.   You're villains, fablers,
  You have knaves' chins and harlots' tongues; you lie,
  And I will damn you with one meal a day!

1. Servant. O good my lord!

Spurio.   'Sblood, you shall never sup!   40

2. Servant. O, I beseech you, sir!

Spurio.   To let my sword
  Catch cold so long and miss him.

1. Servant.   Troth, my lord,
  'Twas his intent to meet there.

Spurio.   Heart, he's yonder.
  Ha? What news here? Is the day out o' th' socket
  That it is noon at midnight? The court up?   45
  How comes the guard so saucy with his elbows?

---

31. *crossed . . . thought*] thwarted more completely than we intended.

33. *fell*] fell out.

36. *Out . . . eye*] out of sight.

38. *harlots'*] rogues' (originally a term applied to men).

  you lie] At II.ii.119 ff. his servants told Spurio that Lussurioso intended to
seduce Castiza this night. The plan has gone awry.

44. *out o' th' socket*] i.e. out of order (the sockets held torches that made it
seem noon).

46. *his*] Lussurioso's, who is under arrest.

Lussurioso. [*Aside*] The bastard here?
    Nay, then, the truth of my intent shall out.
    [*To the Duke*] My lord and father, hear me.
Duke.   Bear him hence.
Lussurioso. I can with loyalty excuse—
Duke.   Excuse?   50
    To prison with the villain!
    Death shall not long lag after him.
Spurio. [*Aside*] Good, i'faith; then 'tis not much amiss.
Lussurioso. Brothers, my best release lies on your tongues;
    I pray persuade for me.
Ambitioso.   It is our duties;   55
    Make yourself sure of us.
Supervacuo.   We'll sweat in pleading.
Lussurioso. And I may live to thank you.   *Exit* [*guarded*].
Ambitioso.   No, thy death
    Shall thank me better.
Spurio. [*Aside*]   He's gone; I'll after him,
    And know his trespass; seem to bear a part
    In all his ills, but with a puritan heart.   *Exit.*   60
Ambitioso. [*Aside to Supervacuo*] Now, brother, let our hate
        and love be woven
    So subtilly together that in speaking
    One word for his life we may make three for his death;
    The craftiest pleader gets most gold for breath.
Supervacuo. [*Aside to Ambitioso*] Set on; I'll not be far behind
        you, brother.   65
Duke. Is 't possible a son should be disobedient as far as the
    sword? It is the highest; he can go no farther.
Ambitioso. My gracious lord, take pity—
Duke.   Pity, boys?
Ambitioso. Nay, we'd be loath to move your grace too much;
    We know the trespass is unpardonable,   70
    Black, wicked, and unnatural—
Supervacuo. In a son, O, monstrous!
Ambitioso.   —yet, my lord,
    A duke's soft hand strokes the rough head of law,
    And makes it lie smooth.
Duke.   But my hand shall ne'er do 't.

---

60. *puritan*] hypocritical.

Ambitioso. That as you please, my lord.

Supervacuo.   We must needs confess   75
    Some father would have entered into hate
    So deadly-pointed that before his eyes
    He would ha' seen the execution sound,
    Without corrupted favour.

Ambitioso.   But my lord,
    Your grace may live the wonder of all times,   80
    In pard'ning that offence which never yet
    Had face to beg a pardon.

Duke. [*Aside*]   Honey? How's this?

Ambitioso. Forgive him, good my lord, he's your own son,—
    And I must needs say, 'twas the vilelier done!

Supervacuo. He's the next heir—yet this true reason gathers: 85
    None can possess that dispossess their fathers.
    Be merciful—

Duke. [*Aside*]   Here's no stepmother's wit;
    I'll try them both upon their love and hate.

Ambitioso. Be merciful—although—

Duke.   You have prevailed;
    My wrath, like flaming wax, hath spent itself.   90
    I know 'twas but some peevish moon in him;
    Go, let him be released.

Supervacuo. [*Aside to Ambitioso*]   'Sfoot, how now, brother?

Ambitioso. Your grace doth please to speak beside your
      spleen;
    I would it were so happy.

Duke.   Why, go, release him.

Supervacuo. O my good lord, I know the fault's too weighty,   95
    And full of general loathing; too inhuman,
    Rather by all men's voices worthy death.

---

78. *sound*] properly carried out.

79. *Without corrupted favour*] i.e. without letting mercy corrupt his judgement.

82. *Honey?*] sweet words, instead of the envy he expects; see l. 104.

87. *stepmother's wit*] the craft of a stepmother (the Duchess), who might be expected to hate Lussurioso, the Duke's heir by a former wife.

91. *peevish moon*] senseless fit of lunacy.

93. *beside your spleen*] leaving your anger aside.

94. *would . . . happy*] i.e. wish the outcome were so fortunate.

Duke. 'Tis true too.
    Here then, receive this signet, doom shall pass;
    Direct it to the judges, he shall die   100
    Ere many days. Make haste.
Ambitioso.   All speed that may be.
    We could have wished his burden not so sore;
    We knew your grace did but delay before.
               Exeunt [AMBITIOSO *and* SUPERVACUO].
Duke. Here's envy with a poor thin cover o'er 't,
    Like scarlet hid in lawn, easily spied through.   105
    This their ambition by the mother's side
    Is dangerous, and for safety must be purged.
    I will prevent their envies; sure it was
    But some mistaken fury in our son,
    Which these aspiring boys would climb upon.   110
    He shall be released suddenly.

             Enter [*two*] Nobles.

1. Noble. Good morning to your grace—
Duke. Welcome, my lords.
2. Noble.   —Our knees shall take
    Away the office of our feet for ever,
    Unless your grace bestow a father's eye   115
    Upon the clouded fortunes of your son,
    And in compassionate virtue grant him that
    Which makes e'en mean men happy,—liberty.
Duke. [*Aside*] How seriously their loves and honours woo
    For that which I am about to pray them do,   120
    Which—[*To them*] rise, my lords; your knees sign his
      release.
    We freely pardon him.
1. Noble. We owe your grace much thanks, and he much duty.
                     Exeunt [Nobles].
Duke. It well becomes that judge to nod at crimes,

---

    99. *signet*] seal, probably in a signet-ring.
    104. *envy*] malice.
    105. *scarlet hid in lawn*] a rich red cloth poorly hidden in transparent fine linen.
    108. *prevent*] forestall.
    111. *suddenly*] at once.

That does commit greater himself and lives;   125
I may forgive a disobedient error,
That expect pardon for adultery,
And in my old days am a youth in lust!
Many a beauty have I turned to poison
In the denial, covetous of all.   130
Age hot is like a monster to be seen;
My hairs are white, and yet my sins are green.   [*Exit.*]

129–30. *turned . . . denial*] caused to be poisoned for rejecting me.
132. *green*] young and fresh.

Act III

ACT III, SCENE i

Enter AMBITIOSO *and* SUPERVACUO.

Supervacuo. Brother, let my opinion sway you once;
    I speak it for the best, to have him die,
    Surest and soonest. If the signet come
    Unto the judges' hands, why then his doom
    Will be deferred till sittings and court-days,   5
    Juries, and further. Faiths are bought and sold;
    Oaths in these days are but the skin of gold.
Ambitioso. In troth, 'tis true too.
Supervacuo.   Then let's set by the judges,
    And fall to the officers; 'tis but mistaking
    The Duke our father's meaning, and where he named   10
    'Ere many days', 'tis but forgetting that,
    And have him die i' th' morning.
Ambitioso.   Excellent!
    Then am I heir—duke in a minute!
Supervacuo. [*Aside*]   Nay,
    An he were once puffed out, here is a pin
    Should quickly prick your bladder!
Ambitioso.   Blest occasion!   15
    He being packed, we'll have some trick and wile
    To wind our younger brother out of prison,
    That lies in for the rape; the lady's dead,
    And people's thoughts will soon be burièd.

III.i.7. *skin of gold*] i.e. a cover for cash transactions.
8. *set by*] disregard.
9. *fall to the officers*] apply to those who have Lussurioso in custody.
14. *An he*] if Lussurioso.
puffed out] 'blown out', like a candle, passing into 'blown up', like a bladder.
a pin] Supervacuo's sword.
16. *packed*] got rid of.

Supervacuo. We may with safety do 't, and live and feed;   20
    The Duchess' sons are too proud to bleed.
Ambitioso. We are, i'faith, to say true. Come, let's not linger.
    I'll to the officers; go you before,
    And set an edge upon the executioner.
Supervacuo. Let me alone to grind him.   *Exit.*
Ambitioso.   Meet! Farewell.   25
    I am next now; I rise just in that place,
    Where thou'rt cut off,—upon thy neck, kind brother.
    The falling of one head lifts up another.   *Exit.*

[III. ii]

      Enter with the Nobles, LUSSURIOSO, *from prison.*

Lussurioso. My lords,
    I am so much indebted to your loves
    For this, O, this delivery.
1. Noble.   But our duties,
    My lord, unto the hopes that grow in you.
Lussurioso. If e'er I live to be myself, I'll thank you.   5
    O Liberty, thou sweet and heavenly dame!—
    But hell for prison is too mild a name.   *Exeunt.*

[III. iii]

      Enter AMBITIOSO *and* SUPERVACUO, *with* Officers.

Ambitioso. Officers,
    Here's the Duke's signet, your firm warrant, brings
    The command of present death along with it
    Unto our brother, the Duke's son. We are sorry
    That we are so unnaturally employed   5
    In such an unkind office, fitter far

---

24. *set . . . executioner*] make the executioner (and his axe) keen.
25. *Meet*] fitting.

III.ii.3. *But*] merely.
5. *myself*] i.e. duke.

III.iii.2. *brings*] that brings.
3. *present*] immediate.
6. *unkind*] (1) cruel (2) unnatural.

For enemies than brothers.
Supervacuo.   But you know
     The Duke's command must be obeyed.
1. Officer. It must, and shall, my lord—this morning, then,
     So suddenly?
Ambitioso.   Ay, alas; poor, good soul,   10
     He must break fast betimes; the executioner
     Stands ready to put forth his cowardly valour.
2. Officer. Already?
Supervacuo. Already, i'faith. O sir, destruction hies,
     And that is least impudent soonest dies.   15
1. Officer. Troth, you say true. My lord, we take our leaves;
     Our office shall be sound, we'll not delay
     The third part of a minute.
Ambitioso.   Therein you show
     Yourselves good men and upright officers.
     Pray let him die as private as he may;   20
     Do him that favour, for the gaping people
     Will but trouble him at his prayers, and make
     Him curse, and swear, and so die black. Will you
     Be so far kind?
1. Officer.   It shall be done, my lord.
Ambitioso. Why, we do thank you; if we live to be,   25
     You shall have a better office.
2. Officer.   Your good lordship.
Supervacuo. Commend us to the scaffold in our tears.
1. Officer. We'll weep, and do your commendations.
                                   Exeunt [Officers].
Ambitioso. Fine fools in office!
Supervacuo.   Things fall out so fit.
Ambitioso. So happily; come, brother; ere next clock,   30
     His head will be made serve a bigger block.   *Exeunt.*

---

14. *hies*] hastens on.
15.] i.e. you need impudence to survive in the court.
17. *sound*] properly carried out.
23. *black*] in sin.
25. *be*] i.e. duke, as he hopes.
31. *block*] executioner's block, quibbling on 'block' = mould for a hat.

[III. iv]

Enter in prison JUNIOR BROTHER.

Junior Brother. Keeper!

[*Enter* Keeper.]

Keeper. My lord.

Junior Brother. No news lately from our brothers?
   Are they unmindful of us?

Keeper. My lord, a messenger came newly in,   5
   And brought this from 'em.   [*Gives him a letter.*]

Junior Brother.   Nothing but paper comforts?
   I looked for my delivery before this,
   Had they been worth their oaths—prithee, be from us.
                              [*Exit* Keeper.]

   Now, what say you, forsooth; speak out, I pray.
                              [*He begins to read the letter.*]

   'Brother, be of good cheer'—'slud, it begins like a whore,   10
   with good cheer; 'thou shalt not be long a prisoner'—not
   five and thirty year, like a bankrupt; I think so! 'We have
   thought upon a device to get thee out by a trick'—by a
   trick? Pox o' your trick, an it be so long a-playing! 'And
   so rest comforted; be merry, and expect it suddenly.' Be   15
   merry! Hang merry, draw and quarter merry; I'll be mad!
   Is 't not strange that a man should lie in a whole month
   for a woman? Well, we shall see how sudden our brothers
   will be in their promise. I must expect still a trick; I shall
   not be long a prisoner.   20

                    [*He tears the letter. Enter* Keeper.]

   How now, what news?

Keeper. Bad news, my lord; I am discharged of you.

Junior Brother. Slave, call'st thou that bad news? I thank you,
   brothers.

   III.iv.10. *'slud*] 'by His (God's) blood'; see I.iii.165.

   13–14. *trick . . . playing*] as if it were a card-game; see ll. 67–8 below.

   15. *suddenly*] at any minute.

   16. *Hang . . . quarter*] treason was punished by hanging, drawing (disembowelling) and quartering.

   17. *lie in*] quibbling on a woman's 'lying in', or confinement at the birth of a child.

Keeper. My lord, 'twill prove so; here come the officers
　　Into whose hands I must commit you.
Junior Brother.　　　　　　　　　　　Ha?　　　　　　25
　　Officers? What, why?

　　　　　　　[*Enter three* Officers.]

1. Officer.　　　　　　You must pardon us, my lord;
　　Our office must be sound. Here is our warrant,
　　The signet from the Duke. You must straight suffer.
Junior Brother. Suffer?
　　I'll suffer you to be gone; I'll suffer you　　　　30
　　To come no more. What would you have me suffer?
2. Officer. My lord, those words were better changed to
　　prayers.
　　The time's but brief with you; prepare to die.
Junior Brother. Sure, 'tis not so!
3. Officer.　　　　　　　　　It is too true, my lord.
Junior Brother. I tell you, 'tis not, for the Duke, my father,　　35
　　Deferred me till next sitting; and I look
　　E'en every minute, threescore times an hour,
　　For a release, a trick wrought by my brothers.
1. Officer. A trick, my lord? If you expect such comfort,
　　Your hope's as fruitless as a barren woman.　　　　40
　　Your brothers were the unhappy messengers
　　That brought this powerful token for your death.
Junior Brother. My brothers? No, no.
2. Officer.　　　　　　　　　　'Tis most true, my lord.
Junior Brother. My brothers to bring a warrant for my death?
　　How strange this shows!
3. Officer.　　　　　　　There's no delaying time.　　45
Junior Brother. Desire 'em hither; call 'em up. My brothers?
　　They shall deny it to your faces.
1. Officer.　　　　　　　　　　My lord,
　　They're far enough by this, at least at court,
　　And this most strict command they left behind 'em;
　　When grief swum in their eyes they showed like brothers,　　50

30-1. *suffer . . . suffer?*] allow (playing on 'suffer pain').
36. *sitting*] session of a court of law.
41. *unhappy*] playing on the meaning 'unlucky' or 'ill-fated'.
50. *showed*] looked.

    Brimfull of heavy sorrow; but the Duke
    Must have his pleasure.
Junior Brother. His pleasure?
1. Officer. These were their last words which my memory
      bears:
    'Commend us to the scaffold in our tears.'   55
Junior Brother. Pox dry their tears; what should I do with
      tears?
    I hate 'em worse than any citizen's son
    Can hate salt water. Here came a letter now
    New-bleeding from their pens, scarce stinted yet—
    Would I'd been torn in pieces when I tore it—   60
    Look, you officious whoresons, words of comfort:
    'Not long a prisoner'.
1. Officer. It says true in that, sir, for you must suffer
      presently.
Junior Brother. [*He finds scraps of the letter.*] A villainous duns
    upon the letter, knavish exposition! Look you then here,   65
    sir: 'We'll get thee out by a trick', says he.
2. Officer. That may hold too, sir, for you know a trick is
    commonly four cards, which was meant by us four offic-
    ers.
Junior Brother. Worse and worse dealing.
1. Officer.   The hour beckons us;   70
    The headsman waits, lift up your eyes to heaven.
Junior Brother. I thank you, faith; good, pretty, wholesome
      counsel;
    I should look up to heaven as you said,
    Whilst he behind cozens me of my head.
    Ay, that's the trick.
3. Officer.   You delay too long, my lord.   75

---

52. *pleasure*] wish, gratification.

58. *salt water*] sea-travel, and alluding perhaps to the custom of pressing
men to serve in the navy.

59. *stinted*] staunched; especially with reference to blood.

64. *duns*] sophistical interpretation; alluding to Duns Scotus, the medieval
theologian famous for his fine distinctions (origin of the modern 'dunce', as
scholastic argument was made to look foolish by the new learning of the
Renaissance).

68. *four cards*] the winning hand in the game of primero was four cards of
the same suit.

Junior Brother. Stay, good authority's bastards; since I must
    Through brothers' perjury die, O let me venom
    Their souls with curses.
1. Officer.   Come, 'tis no time to curse.
Junior Brother. Must I bleed then, without respect of sign?
    Well—   80
    My fault was sweet sport, which the world approves;
    I die for that which every woman loves.   *Exeunt.*

[III. v]

    Enter VINDICE [*in disguise*] *with* HIPPOLITO, *his brother.*

Vindice. O sweet, delectable, rare, happy, ravishing!
Hippolito. Why, what's the matter, brother?
Vindice.   O, 'tis able
    To make a man spring up, and knock his forehead
    Against yon silver ceiling.
Hippolito.   Prithee, tell me,
    Why may not I partake with you? You vowed once   5
    To give me share to every tragic thought.
Vindice. By th' mass, I think I did too.
    Then I'll divide it to thee: the old Duke,
    Thinking my outward shape and inward heart
    Are cut out of one piece (for he that prates   10
    His secrets, his heart stands o' th' outside),
    Hires me by price to greet him with a lady
    In some fit place, veiled from the eyes o' th' court,
    Some darkened, blushless angle, that is guilty
    Of his forefathers' lusts and great folks' riots;   15
    To which I easily (to maintain my shape)
    Consented, and did wish his impudent grace

---

77. *perjury*] broken promises.
79. *bleed . . . sign*] (1) bleed (as if in medical treatment) without a favourable astrological sign (2) be executed without some mark of distinction.

III.v.4. *silver ceiling*] possibly alluding to the 'heavens', or underside of the canopy over the stage at the Globe, painted to look like the sky.
8. *divide it to*] share it with.
14. *angle*] nook or corner.
15. *riots*] wanton revels.

To meet her here in this unsunnèd lodge,
Wherein 'tis night at noon; and here the rather,
Because unto the torturing of his soul   20
The bastard and the Duchess have appointed
Their meeting too in this luxurious circle,
Which most afflicting sight will kill his eyes
Before we kill the rest of him.
Hippolito. 'Twill, i'faith; most dreadfully digested.   25
I see not how you could have missed me, brother.
Vindice. True, but the violence of my joy forgot it.
Hippolito. Ay, but where's that lady now?
Vindice.   O, at that word
I'm lost again, you cannot find me yet;
I'm in a throng of happy apprehensions.   30
He's suited for a lady; I have took care
For a delicious lip, a sparkling eye.
You shall be witness, brother.
Be ready, stand with your hat off.   *Exit.*
Hippolito.   Troth, I wonder
What lady it should be; yet 'tis no wonder,   35
Now I think again, to have a lady
Stoop to a duke, that stoops unto his men.
'Tis common to be common through the world;
And there's more private common shadowing vices
Than those who are known both by their names and
      prices.   40
'Tis part of my allegiance to stand bare

---

18. *unsunnèd lodge*] darkness may have been suggested by the staging at the
Globe, with torches illuminating the stage area where the skull is placed; see
l. 142.
  25. *dreadfully digested*] terrifyingly planned.
  26. *missed me*] left me out, forgot to tell me.
  29. *lost*] i.e. absorbed in the ingenuity of my plan.
  30. *apprehensions*] anticipations.
  34. *with . . . off*] as in the presence of a lady of high rank; see l. 41.
  37. *that stoops*] who degrades himself to the level of.
  38–9. *common*] playing on (1) usual (2) a common woman or harlot (3)
widespread.
  39. *shadowing*] secretive.

To the Duke's concubine,—and here she comes.

Enter VINDICE, *with the skull of his love dressed up in*
tires [and masked].

Vindice. Madam, his grace will not be absent long.
      Secret? Ne'er doubt us, madam; 'twill be worth
      Three velvet gowns to your ladyship. Known?   45
      Few ladies respect that! Disgrace? a poor thin shell;
      'Tis the best grace you have to do it well.
      I'll save your hand that labour; I'll unmask you.
                                            [*Uncovers the skull.*]
Hippolito. Why, brother, brother!
Vindice. Art thou beguiled now? Tut, a lady can,   50
      At such, all hid, beguile a wiser man.
      Have I not fitted the old surfeiter
      With a quaint piece of beauty? Age and bare bone
      Are e'er allied in action. Here's an eye
      Able to tempt a great man—to serve God;   55
      A pretty hanging lip, that has forgot now to dissemble.
      Methinks this mouth should make a swearer tremble,
      A drunkard clasp his teeth, and not undo 'em
      To suffer wet damnation to run through 'em.
      Here's a cheek keeps her colour, let the wind   60
      Go whistle;
      Spout rain, we fear thee not; be hot or cold,
      All's one with us; and is not she absurd,
      Whose fortunes are upon their faces set,
      That fear no other god but wind and wet?   65
Hippolito. Brother, y'have spoke that right.

42.2. tires] = attires; head-dress, veil, wig and mask.
46. *a poor thin shell*] an empty thing, nothing to worry about.
51. *At . . . hid*] i.e. in such a game as hide and seek; 'all hid' is both a name
for this game and a signal cry in it.
53. *quaint*] dainty, fine.
53-4. *Age . . . action*] the Duke (age) and the skull (bone) are allied in the
sense that they use cosmetics and the like to deceive.
59.] to allow the drink that damns him to pass his teeth. Drunkenness is
often condemned as a sin in the Bible, as at Ephesians 5.18.
60-1. *keeps . . . whistle*] that keeps its colour, no matter how hard the wind
blows.
62-5. *Spout . . . wet?*] The skull wears no cosmetics that can be washed
off. The lines echo *King Lear*, III.ii.1 and 14-15.

Is this the form that living shone so bright?
Vindice. The very same.
    And now methinks I could e'en chide myself
    For doting on her beauty, though her death   70
    Shall be revenged after no common action.
    Does the silk-worm expend her yellow labours
    For thee? For thee does she undo herself?
    Are lordships sold to maintain ladyships
    For the poor benefit of a bewitching minute?   75
    Why does yon fellow falsify highways,
    And put his life between the judge's lips,
    To refine such a thing? keeps horse and men
    To beat their valours for her?
    Surely we are all mad people, and they   80
    Whom we think are, are not; we mistake those;
    'Tis we are mad in sense, they but in clothes.
Hippolito. Faith, and in clothes too we, give us our due.
Vindice. Does every proud and self-affecting dame
    Camphor her face for this? and grieve her maker   85
    In sinful baths of milk, when many an infant starves
    For her superfluous outside—all for this?
    Who now bids twenty pound a night, prepares
    Music, perfumes and sweetmeats? All are hushed;
    Thou mayst lie chaste now. It were fine, methinks,   90
    To have thee seen at revels, forgetful feasts,
    And unclean brothels; sure, 'twould fright the sinner,

---

72. *yellow*] the colour of the cocoon it spins, and of gold.

74. *lordships*] estates; see II.i.215–18.

maintain] i.e. in clothes and jewels.

76. *yon fellow*] someone in the audience?

falsify highways] become a highwayman, or turn 'high' ways into morally 'low' ways.

77.] and put himself at the mercy of a judge's sentence.

78. *refine such a thing*] (1) achieve subtler sexual pleasures (2) make more elegant such a thing as a woman (and as the skull he holds).

79. *beat*] exhaust (batter and abate).

83. *clothes too*] as unnecessarily rich and 'superfluous' (l. 87).

84. *self-affecting*] self-loving.

85. *Camphor*] used to perfume soap.

88. *twenty pound*] a large sum, equivalent to hundreds, perhaps even £1000 in today's money.

91. *forgetful*] inducing oblivion.

And make him a good coward, put a reveller
Out of his antic amble,
And cloy an epicure with empty dishes.   95
Here might a scornful and ambitious woman
Look through and through herself;—see, ladies, with
    false forms
You deceive men, but cannot deceive worms.
Now to my tragic business. Look you, brother,
I have not fashioned this only for show   100
And useless property; no, it shall bear a part
E'en in it own revenge. This very skull,
Whose mistress the Duke poisoned, with this drug,
The mortal curse of the earth, shall be revenged
In the like strain, and kiss his lips to death.   105
As much as the dumb thing can, he shall feel:
What fails in poison, we'll supply in steel.

Hippolito. Brother, I do applaud thy constant vengeance,
    The quaintness of thy malice, above thought.

Vindice. [*Putting poison on the lips of the skull*] So, 'tis laid on.
    Now come, and welcome, Duke;   110
I have her for thee. I protest it, brother,
Methinks she makes almost as fair a sign
As some old gentlewoman in a periwig.
                        [*Puts a mask on the skull.*]
Hide thy face now, for shame, thou hadst need have a
    mask now;
'Tis vain when beauty flows, but when it fleets,   115

---

94. *antic amble*] grotesque walk (being drunk).
97. *forms*] appearances. Vindice again speaks to the audience.
101. *property*] playing on the idea of stage property; Vindice is consciously staging his own play. The metaphor continues in 'bear a part'.
102. *it*] its; a common form.
103. *Whose mistress*] the dead Gloriana, whose skull this is.
105. *strain*] manner (literally, melody).
109. *quaintness*] ingenuity.
above thought] more than I can say.
112. *sign*] show or figure.
115–16.] i.e. a mask is mere vanity when beauty exists to be displayed, but when beauty has passed away, 'This' (the skull) better befits the grave than to be shown in public.
115. *flows*] flourishes.
fleets] vanishes, withers away.

This would become graves better than the streets.
Hippolito. You have my voice in that. Hark, the Duke's come.
Vindice. Peace, let's observe what company he brings,
　　And how he does absent 'em, for you know
　　He'll wish all private. Brother, fall you back　　　　　　120
　　A little, with the bony lady.
Hippolito.　　　　　　　　　That I will.
Vindice. So, so—
　　Now nine years' vengeance crowd into a minute!

[*They step aside, as the* Duke *enters, with some* Gentlemen.]

Duke. You shall have leave to leave us, with this charge,
　　Upon your lives: if we be missed by th' Duchess,　　　　125
　　Or any of the nobles, to give out
　　We're privately rid forth.
Vindice. [*Aside*]　　　　　　O happiness!
Duke. With some few honourable gentlemen, you may say;
　　You may name those that are away from court.
Gentlemen. Your will and pleasure shall be done, my lord.　　130
　　　　　　　　　　　　　　　　　　[*Exeunt* Gentlemen.]
Vindice. [*Aside*] 'Privately rid forth';
　　He strives to make sure work on 't! [*To the Duke*] Your
　　good grace.
Duke. Piato, well done, hast brought her? What lady is 't?
Vindice. Faith, my lord, a country lady, a little bashful at first,
　　as most of them are; but after the first kiss, my lord, the　　135
　　worst is past with them. Your grace knows now what you
　　have to do; sh'has somewhat a grave look with her,
　　but—
Duke. I love that best; conduct her.
Vindice. [*Aside*]　　　　　　　　Have at all!

---

117. *You . . . that*] I agree with you.
119. *absent*] send away.
124. *leave to leave*] permission to go (with conscious wordplay).
charge] order, commission.
126–7. *to give . . . forth*] to let it be known that I have secretly gone riding
somewhere.
132. *on 't*] of it.
137. *grave*] the pun on 'grave' as a place of burial is unnoticed by the
Duke, who misses Vindice's mockery.
139. *Have at all!*] on with it! (usually marking the start of a fight).

Duke. In gravest looks the greatest faults seem less.   140
    Give me that sin that's robed in holiness.

Vindice. [*Aside to Hippolito*] Back with the torch; brother, raise
    the perfumes.

Duke. How sweet can a duke breathe? Age has no fault.
    Pleasure should meet in a perfumèd mist.
    Lady, sweetly encountered; I came from court,   145
    I must be bold with you. [*Kisses the skull.*] O, what's this?
    O!

Vindice. Royal villain, white devil!

Duke.   O!

Vindice.   Brother—
    Place the torch here, that his affrighted eyeballs
    May start into those hollows. Duke, dost know
    Yon dreadful vizard? View it well; 'tis the skull   150
    Of Gloriana, whom thou poisonedst last.

Duke. O, 't has poisoned me.

Vindice. Didst not know that till now?

Duke.   What are you two?

Vindice. Villains all three! The very ragged bone
    Has been sufficiently revenged.   155

Duke. O, Hippolito! Call treason.

Hippolito. Yes, my good lord; treason, treason, treason!
                          Stamping on him.

Duke. Then I'm betrayed.

Vindice. Alas, poor lecher, in the hands of knaves,
    A slavish duke is baser than his slaves.   160

Duke. My teeth are eaten out.

Vindice.   Hadst any left?

Hippolito. I think but few.

142.] Vindice wants less light on the skull, and a mist of perfume (l. 144; from the Latin *fumare*, to smoke) to confuse and entice the Duke.

143. *no fault*] no physical inadequacy (and also playing on the idea of moral defect).

147. *white*] white-haired, and fair-seeming (a 'white devil' was a hypocrite, the worst kind of devil proverbially, as in John Webster's play, *The White Devil*).

151. *last*] see II.iii.129–30.

154. *all three*] Vindice, Hippolito and either the Duke or Gloriana.
ragged] rough, jagged.

160. *slavish*] (1) vile (2) forced into submission.

Vindice. Then those that did eat are eaten.

Duke.　　　　　　　　　　　　　　　O, my tongue!

Vindice. Your tongue? 'Twill teach you to kiss closer,
　　　Not like a slobbering Dutchman. You have eyes still, 165
　　　Look, monster, what a lady hast thou made me
　　　My once betrothèd wife.　　　[*Throwing off his disguise.*]

Duke.　　　　　　　　　　　Is it thou, villain?
　　　Nay then—

Vindice.　　　　'Tis I, 'tis Vindice, 'tis I.

Hippolito. And let this comfort thee: our lord and father
　　　Fell sick upon the infection of thy frowns, 170
　　　And died in sadness; be that thy hope of life.

Duke. O!

Vindice. He had his tongue, yet grief made him die speechless.
　　　Puh, 'tis but early yet, now I'll begin
　　　To stick thy soul with ulcers. I will make 175
　　　Thy spirit grievous sore; it shall not rest,
　　　But, like some pestilent man, toss in thy breast—
　　　Mark me, Duke:
　　　Thou'rt a renownèd, high and mighty cuckold.

Duke. O!　　　　　　　　　　　　　　　　　　　180

Vindice. Thy bastard,
　　　Thy bastard rides a-hunting in thy brow.

Duke. Millions of deaths!

Vindice.　　　　　　　　　Nay, to afflict thee more,
　　　Here in this lodge they meet for damnèd clips;
　　　Those eyes shall see the incest of their lips. 185

Duke. Is there a hell besides this, villains?

Vindice.　　　　　　　　　　　　　　　Villain!
　　　Nay, Heaven is just, scorns are the hires of scorns;
　　　I ne'er knew yet adulterer without horns.

Hippolito. Once e'er they die 'tis quitted.

Vindice.　　　　　　　　　　　　　Hark, the music;

---

165. *Dutchman*] proverbially noted for drunkenness, hence slobbering.

166. *made me*] made for me.

177. *pestilent*] infected with the plague.

182. *rides . . . brow*] for the sexual implications, compare I.ii.136–8; and see I.ii.4 and n.

184. *clips*] embraces.

187. *hires*] rewards.

189. *Once*] at least once.
　quitted] requited.

Their banquet is prepared, they're coming—   190
Duke. O, kill me not with that sight!
Vindice. Thou shalt not lose that sight for all thy dukedom.
Duke. Traitors, murderers!
Vindice. What? Is not thy tongue eaten out yet? Then
    We'll invent a silence. Brother, stifle the torch.   195
Duke. Treason, murder!
Vindice. Nay, faith, we'll have you hushed. [*To Hippolito*]
        Now with thy dagger
    Nail down his tongue, and mine shall keep possession
    About his heart. If he but gasp, he dies.
    We dread not death to quittance injuries.   200
    Brother,
    If he but wink, not brooking the foul object,
    Let our two other hands tear up his lids,
    And make his eyes, like comets, shine through blood;
    When the bad bleeds, then is the tragedy good.   205
Hippolito. Whist, brother, music's at our ear; they come.

Enter the Bastard [SPURIO] *meeting the* Duchess. [*They kiss.*
        Attendants *with lights stand apart.*]

Spurio. Had not that kiss a taste of sin, 'twere sweet.
Duchess. Why, there's no pleasure sweet but it is sinful.
Spurio. True, such a bitter sweetness fate hath given,
    Best side to us is the worst side to heaven.   210
Duchess. Push, come; 'tis the old Duke thy doubtful father;
    The thought of him rubs heaven in thy way.
    But I protest, by yonder waxen fire,
    Forget him, or I'll poison him.

---

195. *invent*] establish.
198–9. *Nail . . . heart*] i.e. to stop him talking, and threaten him with instant death.
200. *quittance*] repay.
202. *wink*] blink.
brooking] enduring.
object] what is before his eyes, i.e. Spurio and the Duchess embracing.
207. *kiss*] paralleling the Duke kissing the skull at l. 146.
211. *doubtful*] questionable; see I.ii.134.
212. *rubs*] brings to mind as a stumbling block; a 'rub' is an obstacle in the game of bowls.
213. *waxen fire*] torches.

Spurio. Madam, you urge a thought which ne'er had life.   215
    So deadly do I loathe him for my birth
    That if he took me hasped within his bed,
    I would add murder to adultery,
    And with my sword give up his years to death.
Duchess. Why, now thou'rt sociable; let's in, and feast.   220
    Loud'st music sound! Pleasure is banquet's guest.
                Exeunt [Duchess, SPURIO *and* Attendants].
Duke. I cannot brook—   [*Dies.*]
Vindice.   The brook is turned to blood.
Hippolito. Thanks to loud music.
Vindice.   'Twas our friend indeed.
    'Tis state in music for a duke to bleed.
    The dukedom wants a head, though yet unknown;   225
    As fast as they peep up, let's cut 'em down.   *Exeunt.*

[III. vi]

    Enter the Duchess's two sons, AMBITIOSO *and* SUPERVACUO.

Ambitioso. Was not his execution rarely plotted?
    We are the Duke's sons now.
Supervacuo.   Ay, you may thank
    My policy for that.
Ambitioso.   Your policy?
    For what?
Supervacuo.   Why, was 't not my invention, brother,
    To slip the judges? And, in lesser compass,   5
    Did I not draw the model of his death,

---

215. *ne'er had life*] never became conscious.

217. *hasped*] in the act of incest.

222. *brook*] put up with (verb), and stream (noun).

224.] i.e. it is appropriately ceremonial for a duke to die while music is played.

225. *unknown*] i.e. not public knowledge.

226. *they*] other heirs and claimants to the dukedom.

III.vi.1. *execution*] Lussurioso's, as they think; and, ironically, the Duke's.

3. *policy*] stratagem.

5. *slip*] bypass.

compass] scope; suggesting also the drawing instrument (now 'compasses').

6. *model*] plan.

Advising you to sudden officers,
And e'en extemporal execution?

Ambitioso. Heart, 'twas a thing I thought on too.

Supervacuo. You thought on 't too? 'Sfoot, slander not your
    thoughts   10
With glorious untruth; I know 'twas from you.

Ambitioso. Sir,
I say 'twas in my head.

Supervacuo.   Ay, like your brains then;
Ne'er to come out as long as you lived.

Ambitioso. You'd have the honour on 't, forsooth, that your
    wit   15
Led him to the scaffold.

Supervacuo.   Since it is my due,
I'll publish 't, but I'll ha 't in spite of you.

Ambitioso. Methinks y'are much too bold; you should a little
Remember us, brother, next to be honest duke.

Supervacuo. Ay, it shall be as easy for you to be duke   20
As to be honest; and that's never, i'faith.

Ambitioso. Well, cold he is by this time; and because
We're both ambitious, be it our amity,
And let the glory be shared equally.

Supervacuo. I am content to that.   25

Ambitioso. This night our younger brother shall out of prison;
I have a trick.

Supervacuo.   A trick, prithee what is 't?

Ambitioso. We'll get him out by a wile.

Supervacuo.   Prithee what wile?

Ambitioso. No, sir, you shall not know it till 't be done,
For then you'd swear 'twere yours.   30

[*Enter an* Officer.]

---

7. *sudden*] unlooked for, and swift in action.

8. *extemporal*] immediate.

9. *Heart*] i.e. by God's heart (an oath).
on] of.

11. *from you*] not in your thoughts.

19.] i.e. remember, brother, that I am next in line to be honoured duke
(he already uses the royal plural 'us'). In l. 21 Supervacuo plays sarcastically
on 'honest' in the senses of 'truth-telling' and 'virtuous'.

22. *he*] Lussurioso.

Supervacuo. How now, what's he?

Ambitioso.   One of the officers.

Supervacuo. Desirèd news.

Ambitioso.   How now, my friend?

Officer.   My lords,
    Under your pardon, I am allotted
    To that desertless office, to present you
    With the yet bleeding head—

Supervacuo. [Aside]   Ha, ha, excellent!   35

Ambitioso. [Aside] All's sure our own. Brother, canst weep,
    think'st thou?
    'Twould grace our flattery much; think of some dame,
    'Twill teach thee to dissemble.

Supervacuo. [Aside]   I have thought;
    Now for yourself.   [*They pretend to weep.*]

Ambitioso.   Our sorrows are so fluent,
    Our eyes o'erflow our tongues. Words spoke in tears   40
    Are like the murmurs of the waters; the sound
    Is loudly heard, but cannot be distinguished.

Supervacuo. How died he, pray?

Officer.   O, full of rage and spleen.

Supervacuo. He died most valiantly then; we're glad
    To hear it.

Officer.   We could not woo him once to pray.   45

Ambitioso. He showed himself a gentleman in that,
    Give him his due.

Officer.   But in the stead of prayer,
    He drew forth oaths.

Supervacuo.   Then did he pray, dear heart,
    Although you understood him not.

Officer.   My lords,
    E'en at his last, with pardon be it spoke,   50
    He cursed you both.

---

32. *Desirèd news*] here's welcome news. (He expects news of Lussurioso's death; the news he gets is not so welcome.)

37. *'Twould . . . much*] it would make our show of sorrow more convincing.

37–8. *think . . . dissemble*] proverbially to 'play the woman' was to dissemble; see ll. 83–4.

50. *with pardon be it spoke*] pardon me for saying it.

Supervacuo.   He cursed us? 'Las, good soul!
Ambitioso. It was not in our powers, but the Duke's pleasure.
    [*Aside*] Finely dissembled o' both sides. Sweet fate!
    O, happy opportunity!

                    Enter LUSSURIOSO.

Lussurioso.   Now, my lords.
Both. O!—
Lussurioso.   Why do you shun me, brothers? You may   55
    Come nearer now;
    The savour of the prison has forsook me.
    I thank such kind lords as yourselves, I'm free.
Ambitioso. Alive!
Supervacuo. In health!   60
Ambitioso. Released?
    We were both e'en amazed with joy to see it.
Lussurioso. I am much to thank you.
Supervacuo. Faith,
    We spared no tongue unto my lord the Duke.   65
Ambitioso. I know your delivery, brother,
    Had not been half so sudden but for us.
Supervacuo. O, how we pleaded!
Lussurioso.   Most deserving brothers!
    In my best studies I will think of it.   *Exit.*
Ambitioso. O death and vengeance!
Supervacuo.   Hell and torments!   70
Ambitioso. Slave, cam'st thou to delude us?
Officer.   Delude you, my lords?
Supervacuo. Ay, villain, where's this head now?
Officer.   Why, here, my lord;
    Just after his delivery, you both came
    With warrant from the Duke to behead your brother.
Ambitioso. Ay, our brother, the Duke's son.
Officer.   The Duke's son,   75
    My lord, had his release before you came.
Ambitioso. Whose head's that, then?
Officer.   His whom you left command for,

---

73. *his delivery*] the release of Lussurioso from prison (see III.ii).

Your own brother's.
Ambitioso.   Our brother's? O furies!
Supervacuo. Plagues!
Ambitioso.   Confusions!
Supervacuo.   Darkness!
Ambitioso.   Devils!
Supervacuo. Fell it out so accursedly?
Ambitioso.   So damnedly?   80
Supervacuo. Villain, I'll brain thee with it.
Officer.   O, my good lord.   [*Exit.*]
Supervacuo. The devil overtake thee!
Ambitioso.   O, fatal!
Supervacuo. O, prodigious to our bloods!
Ambitioso.   Did we dissemble?
Supervacuo. Did we make our tears women for thee?
Ambitioso. Laugh and rejoice for thee?   85
Supervacuo. Bring warrant for thy death?
Ambitioso.   Mock off thy head?
Supervacuo. You had a trick, you had a wile, forsooth!
Ambitioso. A murrain meet 'em, there's none of these wiles
     that ever come to good. I see now, there is nothing sure
     in mortality but mortality.   90
     Well, no more words, 'shalt be revenged i'faith.
     Come, throw off clouds now, brother, think of
          vengeance,
     And deeper settled hate. Sirrah, sit fast,
     We'll pull down all, but thou shalt down at last.
                                              Exeunt.

---

83. *prodigious*] ominous.
84. *tears women*] see ll. 37–8 and n.
84–6. *for thee . . . thy head?*] referring to Lussurioso, who left at l. 69.
88. *murrain*] plague.
90. *in mortality but mortality*] in mortal existence except death.
92. *clouds*] of melancholy.
93. *Sirrah*] contemptuously referring to Lussurioso.

Act IV

Enter LUSSURIOSO, *with* HIPPOLITO.

Lussurioso. Hippolito.
Hippolito.   My lord, has your good lordship aught
    To command me in?
Lussurioso.   I prithee leave us.
Hippolito.   How's this?
    Come, and leave us?
Lussurioso.   Hippolito.
Hippolito.   Your honour,
    I stand ready for any duteous employment.
Lussurioso. Heart, what mak'st thou here?
Hippolito. [*Aside*]   A pretty lordly humour;   5
    He bids me to be present, to depart.
    Something has stung his honour.
Lussurioso.   Be nearer, draw nearer;
    Y'are not so good, methinks; I'm angry with you.
Hippolito. With me, my lord? I'm angry with myself for 't.
Lussurioso. You did prefer a goodly fellow to me;   10
    'Twas wittily elected, 'twas. I thought
    'Had been a villain, and he proves a knave,
    To me a knave.
Hippolito.   I chose him for the best, my lord;
    'Tis much my sorrow, if neglect in him
    Breed discontent in you.
Lussurioso.   Neglect? 'Twas will.   15
    Judge of it:
    Firmly to tell of an incredible act,
    Not to be thought, less to be spoken of,

IV.i.8. *not so good*] not so clever after all; see II.ii.1–2.
11. *wittily elected*] wisely chosen (said sarcastically).
14. *neglect in him*] i.e. neglect of his duty to you.
15. *will*] intent, wilfulness.

'Twixt my stepmother and the bastard, O,
Incestuous sweets between 'em.

Hippolito.   Fie, my lord.   20

Lussurioso. I, in kind loyalty to my father's forehead,
    Made this a desperate arm, and in that fury
    Committed treason on the lawful bed,
    And with my sword e'en razed my father's bosom,
    For which I was within a stroke of death.   25

Hippolito. Alack, I'm sorry. [*Aside*] 'Sfoot, just upon the stroke
    Jars in my brother; 'twill be villainous music.

Enter VINDICE *in disguise.*

Vindice. My honoured lord.

Lussurioso. Away, prithee forsake us; hereafter we'll not know
    thee.

Vindice. Not know me, my lord? Your lordship cannot
    choose.   30

Lussurioso. Be gone, I say; thou art a false knave.

Vindice. Why, the easier to be known, my lord.

Lussurioso. Push, I shall prove too bitter, with a word
    Make thee a perpetual prisoner,
    And lay this iron-age upon thee.

Vindice. [*Aside*]   Mum!   35
    For there's a doom would make a woman dumb.
    Missing the bastard, next him, the wind's come about;
    Now 'tis my brother's turn to stay, mine to go out.

                               Exit.

Lussurioso. 'Has greatly moved me.

Hippolito.   Much to blame, i'faith.

Lussurioso. But I'll recover, to his ruin. 'Twas told me lately,   40

---

21. *forehead*] see II.ii.162–3.

24. *razed*] scratched.

27. *Jars in*] comes in discordantly.

30. *cannot choose*] cannot help but know me.

35. *iron-age*] fetters or imprisonment (compare IV.ii.133); also the last and worst of the mythical four ages (Gold, Silver, Brazen, and Iron), an age of cruelty and evil.

36. *woman dumb*] women proverbially were unable to stop talking.

37. *Missing . . . him*] i.e. since I have failed to bring about the deaths of Spurio or of Lussurioso.

I know not whether falsely, that you'd a brother.

Hippolito. Who, I? Yes, my good lord, I have a brother.

Lussurioso. How chance the court ne'er saw him? Of what
    nature?

How does he apply his hours?

Hippolito.   Faith, to curse fates,

Who, as he thinks, ordained him to be poor;   45

Keeps at home, full of want and discontent.

Lussurioso. There's hope in him, for discontent and want

Is the best clay to mould a villain of.

Hippolito, wish him repair to us.

If there be aught in him to please our blood,   50

For thy sake we'll advance him, and build fair

His meanest fortunes; for it is in us

To rear up towers from cottages.

Hippolito.   It is so, my lord.

He will attend your honour; but he's a man

In whom much melancholy dwells.

Lussurioso.   Why, the better.   55

Bring him to court.

Hippolito.   With willingness, and speed.

  [*Aside*] Whom he cast off e'en now, must now succeed.

Brother, disguise must off;

In thine own shape now I'll prefer thee to him.

How strangely does himself work to undo him.   *Exit.*   60

Lussurioso. This fellow will come fitly; he shall kill

That other slave, that did abuse my spleen,

And made it swell to treason. I have put

Much of my heart into him; he must die.

He that knows great men's secrets and proves slight,   65

---

49. *wish . . . to us*] bid him come to me.

50. *blood*] temper.

52–3. *His . . . cottages*] i.e. his worst state of fortune, for it is in my power
to raise the lowly to great heights.

57. *succeed*] be the successor, and be successful.

62. *other slave*] i.e. Piato.

spleen] anger.

63. *to treason*] i.e. to the point of drawing my sword on the Duke, a
treasonous act.

63–4. *put . . . him*] confided too much in him.

65. *slight*] untrustworthy.

That man ne'er lives to see his beard turn white.
Ay, he shall speed him; I'll employ the brother.
Slaves are but nails, to drive out one another.
He being of black condition, suitable
To want and ill content, hope of preferment   70
Will grind him to an edge.

Enter [two] Nobles.

1. Noble. Good days unto your honour.
Lussurioso. My kind lords, I do return the like.
2. Noble. Saw you my lord the Duke?
Lussurioso. My lord and father? Is he from court?   75
1. Noble. He's sure from court; but where, which way his
    pleasure took, we know not, nor can we hear on 't.
Lussurioso. Here come those should tell.

[Enter two more Nobles.]

    Saw you my lord and father?
3. Noble. Not since two hours before noon, my lord; and then 80
    he privately rid forth.
Lussurioso. O, he's rode forth.
1. Noble.   'Twas wondrous privately.
2. Noble. There's none i' th' court had any knowledge on 't.
Lussurioso. His grace is old, and sudden; 'tis no treason
    To say the Duke my father has a humour,   85
    Or such a toy about him. What in us
    Would appear light, in him seems virtuous.
3. Noble. 'Tis oracle, my lord.   *Exeunt.*

[IV. ii]

Enter VINDICE *and* HIPPOLITO, *Vindice out of his disguise.*

Hippolito. So, so, all's as it should be, y'are yourself.

---

    67. *he shall speed him*] Vindice shall kill him (i.e. Piato, his first disguise).
    69. *black*] melancholic.
    70. *want*] poverty.
    78. *should*] who should be able to.
    84. *sudden*] i.e. acts on impulse.
    85. *humour*] caprice.
    86. *toy*] whim.
    87. *light*] frivolous.
    88. *oracle*] absolute truth.

Vindice. How that great villain puts me to my shifts.
Hippolito. He that did lately in disguise reject thee,
    Shall, now thou art thyself, as much respect thee.
Vindice. 'Twill be the quainter fallacy. But, brother,   5
    'Sfoot, what use will he put me to now, think'st thou?
Hippolito. Nay, you must pardon me in that; I know not.
    'Has some employment for you, but what 'tis,
    He and his secretary the devil knows best.
Vindice. Well, I must suit my tongue to his desires,   10
    What colour soe'er they be; hoping at last
    To pile up all my wishes on his breast.
Hippolito. Faith, brother, he himself shows the way.
Vindice. Now the Duke is dead, the realm is clad in clay;
    His death being not yet known, under his name   15
    The people still are governed. Well, thou his son
    Art not long-lived; thou shall not joy his death.
    To kill thee, then, I should most honour thee,
    For 'twould stand firm in every man's belief
    Thou'st a kind child, and only died'st with grief.   20
Hippolito. You fetch about well, but let's talk in present.
    How will you appear in fashion different,
    As well as in apparel, to make all things possible?
    If you be but once tripped, we fall for ever.
    It is not the least policy to be doubtful;   25
    You must change tongue—familiar was your first.
Vindice. Why,
    I'll bear me in some strain of melancholy,
    And string myself with heavy-sounding wire,

IV.ii.2. *shifts*] tricks and disguises.
5. *quainter fallacy*] more ingenious deception.
12. *pile . . . breast*] i.e. press him to death.
14.] Vindice appears to mean that with the death of the Duke no one has power, and the old regime is 'clad in clay', or dead and buried.
16. *thou*] invoking the absent Lussurioso.
17. *joy*] enjoy.
20. *Thou'st*] thou wast.
21. *fetch about*] take a circuitous course.
in present] i.e. about what's to be done now.
25.] i.e. it's not a bad idea to be cautious.
26.] i.e. you must change your manner of speech; your first was too free and unceremonious (see I.iii.37).

Like such an instrument that speaks   30
   Merry things sadly.
Hippolito.   Then 'tis as I meant;
   I gave you out at first in discontent.
Vindice. I'll turn myself, and then—
Hippolito.   'Sfoot, here he comes;
   Hast thought upon 't?
Vindice.   Salute him; fear not me.

       [*Enter* LUSSURIOSO. *Vindice stands apart.*]

Lussurioso. Hippolito.
Hippolito.   Your lordship?
Lussurioso.   What's he yonder?   35
Hippolito. 'Tis Vindice, my discontented brother,
   Whom, 'cording to your will, I've brought to court.
Lussurioso. Is that thy brother? Beshrew me, a good presence;
   I wonder 'has been from the court so long.—
   Come nearer.   40
Hippolito. Brother, Lord Lussurioso, the Duke's son.
              [*Vindice, approaching,*] *snatches off his hat,*
              and makes legs to him. [*Hippolito stands*
              apart.]
Lussurioso. Be more near to us. Welcome; nearer yet.
Vindice. How don you? God you god den.
Lussurioso.   We thank thee.
   How strangely such a coarse, homely salute
   Shows in the palace, where we greet in fire;   45
   Nimble and desperate tongues, should we name God
   In a salutation, 'twould ne'er be stood on 't; heaven!
   Tell me, what has made thee so melancholy?

32.] from the start I reported you to be discontented; see IV.i.46.

33. *turn*] transform.

38. *Beshrew me*] may evil befall me (a common imprecation); often used casually, but here with ironic effect.

presence] demeanour or appearance.

41.2. legs] i.e. 'scrapes', or bows made by drawing back one leg and bending the other.

43. *How . . . den*] i.e. How do you do? God give you good even; Vindice puts on a rustic mode of speech.

46. *desperate*] reckless.

47. *'twould . . . on 't*] no one would bother about it.

Vindice. Why, going to law.

Lussurioso. Why, will that make man melancholy?   50

Vindice. Yes, to look long upon ink and black buckram. I
          went me to law in *anno quadragesimo secundo*, and I waded
          out of it in *anno sexagesimo tertio*.

Lussurioso. What, three and twenty years in law?

Vindice. I have known those that have been five and fifty, and   55
          all about pullen and pigs.

Lussurioso. May it be possible such men should breathe, to
          vex the terms so much?

Vindice. 'Tis food to some, my lord. There are old men at the
          present that are so poisoned with the affectation of law-   60
          words (having had many suits canvassed) that their com-
          mon talk is nothing but Barbary Latin. They cannot so
          much as pray but in law, that their sins may be removed
          with a writ of error, and their souls fetched up to
          heaven with a sasarara.   65

Lussurioso. It seems most strange to me,
          Yet all the world meets round in the same bent;
          Where the heart's set, there goes the tongue's consent.
          How dost apply thy studies, fellow?

Vindice. Study? Why, to think how a great rich man lies a-   70
          dying, and a poor cobbler tolls the bell for him; how he
          cannot depart the world, and sees the great chest stand
          before him when he lies speechless; how he will point you
          readily to all the boxes, and when he is past all memory,

---

52. *went me to law*] entered on a lawsuit.

52–3. anno . . . tertio] the 42nd and 63rd years (usually of a ruler's reign).

56. *pullen*] poultry.

58. *the terms*] the four terms of law-court sessions.

61. *canvassed*] brought for investigation.

62. *Barbary*] outlandish, barbarous.

64. *a writ of error*] a writ brought to reverse a judgement, on grounds of error.

65. *sasarara*] from Latin 'certiorari', a writ issued in a superior court (here the court of God) on the complaint of someone who has not received justice in an inferior court.

67.] i.e. yet people everywhere follow the same course or tendency. 'Bent' also suggests the curving 'round' of the globe.

68.] varying the proverb, 'What the heart thinks the tongue speaks.'

72. *great chest*] where his money and documents are kept.

as the gossips guess, then thinks he of forfeitures and   75
obligations; nay, when to all men's hearings he whurls
and rattles in the throat, he's busy threatening his
poor tenants; and this would last me now some seven
years' thinking, or thereabouts. But I have a conceit a-
coming in picture upon this, I draw it myself; which,   80
i'faith la, I'll present to your honour. You shall not
choose but like it, for your lordship shall give me nothing
for it.

Lussurioso. Nay, you mistake me then,
          For I am published bountiful enough.   85
          Let's taste of your conceit.

Vindice. In picture, my lord—

Lussurioso. Ay, in picture.

Vindice. Marry, this it is—A usuring father to be boiling in
          hell, and his son and heir with a whore dancing over   90
          him.

Hippolito. [*Aside*] 'Has pared him to the quick.

Lussurioso. The conceit's pretty, i'faith; but, take 't upon my
          life, 'twill ne'er be liked.

Vindice. No? Why, I'm sure the whore will be liked well   95
          enough.

Hippolito. [*Aside*] Ay, if she were out o' th' picture, he'd like
          her then himself.

Vindice. And as for the son and heir, he shall be an eyesore to
          no young revellers, for he shall be drawn in cloth of gold   100
          breeches.

Lussurioso. And thou hast put my meaning in the pockets,
          And canst not draw that out. My thought was this:
          To see the picture of a usuring father
          Boiling in hell, our rich men would ne'er like it.   105

75–6. *forfeitures and obligations*] legal terms: losses of goods or lands, and
bonds for the payment of money, with penalties for non-payment.

76. *whurls*] rumbles.

79–80. *conceit . . . this*] witty device picturing itself in my imagination.

85. *published*] reputed.

97. *out o' th' picture*] i.e. here in flesh and blood, not merely in
imagination.

102–3. *thou . . . out*] i.e. you have put my intended bounty (see l. 85) in the
pockets, and will get nothing from me. (Lussurioso correctly sees himself in
the pictured 'son and heir', but as usual misses Vindice's irony.)

Vindice. O true, I cry you heartily mercy; I know the reason,
   for some of 'em had rather be damned indeed than
   damned in colours.

Lussurioso. [*Aside*] A parlous melancholy! 'Has wit enough
   To murder any man, and I'll give him means:—   110
   [*To him*] I think thou art ill-monied.

Vindice.   Money? Ho, ho,
   'T has been my want so long, 'tis now my scoff.
   I've e'en forgot what colour silver's of.

Lussurioso. [*Aside*] It hits as I could wish.

Vindice.   I get good clothes
   Of those that dread my humour, and for table-room,   115
   I feed on those that cannot be rid of me.

Lussurioso. Somewhat to set thee up withal.

                                      [*Gives him money.*]

Vindice. O, mine eyes!

Lussurioso.   How now, man?

Vindice.   Almost struck blind;
   This bright unusual shine to me seems proud;
   I dare not look till the sun be in a cloud.   120

Lussurioso. I think I shall affect his melancholy.
   How are they now?

Vindice.   The better for your asking.

Lussurioso. You shall be better yet, if you but fasten
   Truly on my intent. [*Beckons to Hippolito.*] Now y'are
      both present,
   I will unbrace such a close, private villain   125
   Unto your vengeful swords, the like ne'er heard of,
   Who hath disgraced you much, and injured us.

Hippolito. Disgraced us, my lord?

Lussurioso.   Ay, Hippolito.

---

106. *cry you . . . mercy*] beg your pardon.

108. *in colours*] in a painting.

109. *parlous*] shrewd, biting.

114-16. *I get . . . of me*] i.e. those who fear my melancholy and morbid wit
give me clothes to be rid of me (hence my handsome appearance, l. 38), while
I get meals ('table-room') from those who cannot shake me off.

121. *affect*] like.

125. *unbrace*] reveal (literally, undress, ironic in relation to Vindice's
disguise).

    I kept it here till now that both your angers
    Might meet him at once.
Vindice.   I'm covetous   130
    To know the villain.
Lussurioso.   You know him, that slave-pander,
    Piato, whom we threatened last
    With irons in perpetual prisonment.
Vindice. [*Aside*] All this is I.
Hippolito.   Is 't he, my lord?
Lussurioso.   I'll tell you,
    You first preferred him to me.
Vindice.   Did you, brother?   135
Hippolito. I did indeed.
Lussurioso.   And the ingrateful villain,
    To quit that kindness, strongly wrought with me,
    Being, as you see, a likely man for pleasure,
    With jewels to corrupt your virgin sister.
Hippolito. O, villain!
Vindice.   He shall surely die that did it.   140
Lussurioso. I, far from thinking any virgin harm,
    Especially knowing her to be as chaste
    As that part which scarce suffers to be touched,
    Th' eye, would not endure him.
Vindice.   Would you not,
    My lord? 'Twas wondrous honourably done.   145
Lussurioso. But with some fine frowns kept him out.
Vindice.   Out, slave!
Lussurioso. What did me he, but, in revenge of that,
    Went of his own free will to make infirm
    Your sister's honour, whom I honour with my soul,
    For chaste respect; and not prevailing there   150
    (As 'twas but desperate folly to attempt it),
    In mere spleen, by the way, waylays your mother,
    Whose honour being a coward, as it seems,

---

129. *here*] gesturing to his head or heart to show he has kept it secret.
137. *quit*] repay.
   wrought with me] pressured me ('wrought' is a form of the past participle 'worked').
147. *What did me he*] what did he do ('me' = 'mark me' or 'I tell you').
150. *For chaste respect*] out of regard for chastity.

Yielded by little force.

Vindice.   Coward indeed!

Lussurioso. He, proud of this advantage (as he thought),   155
  Brought me these news for happy; but I, heaven
  Forgive me for 't—

Vindice. What did your honour?

Lussurioso.   In rage pushed him from me,
  Trampled beneath his throat, spurned him, and bruised;
  Indeed, I was too cruel, to say troth.   160

Hippolito. Most nobly managed.

Vindice. [*Aside*]   Has not heaven an ear?
  Is all the lightning wasted?

Lussurioso.   If I now
  Were so impatient in a modest cause,
  What should you be?

Vindice.   Full mad; he shall not live
  To see the moon change.

Lussurioso.   He's about the palace.   165
  Hippolito, entice him this way, that thy brother may take
  full mark of him.

Hippolito. Heart, that shall not need, my lord. I can direct him
  so far.

Lussurioso. Yet, for my hate's sake, go, wind him this way; I'll   170
  see him bleed myself.

Hippolito. [*Aside*] What now, brother?

Vindice. [*Aside*] Nay, e'en what you will; y'are put to't,
    brother.

Hippolito. [*Aside*] An impossible task, I'll swear,
  To bring him hither that's already here.   *Exit.*   175

Lussurioso. Thy name, I have forgot it.

Vindice.   Vindice, my lord.

Lussurioso. 'Tis a good name, that.

Vindice.   Ay, a revenger.

Lussurioso. It does betoken courage; thou shouldst be valiant,

---

156. *for happy*] i.e. as showing his success.
159. *spurned*] kicked.
163. *modest*] limited, small.
166–7. *take . . . of him*] observe him well.
170. *wind*] entice.
173. *y'are put to 't*] you are on your mettle, driven to extremity.

And kill thine enemies.
Vindice.   That's my hope, my lord.
Lussurioso. This slave is one.
Vindice.   I'll doom him.
Lussurioso.   Then I'll praise thee;   180
Do thou observe me best, and I'll best raise thee.

Enter HIPPOLITO.

Vindice. Indeed, I thank you.
Lussurioso.   Now, Hippolito,
Where's the slave-pander?
Hippolito.   Your good lordship would have
A loathsome sight of him, much offensive.
He's not in case now to be seen, my lord;   185
The worst of all the deadly sins is in him,
That beggarly damnation, drunkenness.
Lussurioso. Then he's a double slave.
Vindice. [*Aside*]   'Twas well conveyed,
Upon a sudden wit.
Lussurioso.   What, are you both
Firmly resolved? I'll see him dead myself.   190
Vindice. Or else let not us live.
Lussurioso.   You may direct
Your brother to take note of him.
Vindice.   I shall.
Lussurioso. Rise but in this, and you shall never fall.
Vindice. Your honour's vassals.
Lussurioso. [*Aside*]   This was wisely carried;
Deep policy in us makes fools of such: 195
Then must a slave die, when he knows too much.

Exit.

Vindice. O, thou almighty patience! 'Tis my wonder
That such a fellow, impudent and wicked,
Should not be cloven as he stood, or with

---

180. *This slave*] i.e. Piato.
181. *observe*] humour or please.
185. *in case*] in a condition; quibbling on 'case' = clothes or disguise.
188. *conveyed*] managed.
189. *wit*] device.
199. *cloven*] split in two.

A secret wind burst open.   200
Is there no thunder left, or is 't kept up
In stock for heavier vengeance? There it goes!
                                        [*Thunder sounds.*]
Hippolito. Brother, we lose ourselves.
Vindice.   But I have found it;
  'Twill hold, 'tis sure; thanks, thanks to any spirit
  That mingled it 'mongst my inventions.   205
Hippolito. What is 't?
Vindice.   'Tis sound, and good; thou shalt partake it.
  I'm hired to kill myself.
Hippolito.   True.
Vindice.   Prithee mark it;
  And the old Duke being dead, but not conveyed,
  For he's already missed, too, and you know,
  Murder will peep out of the closest husk.   210
Hippolito. Most true.
Vindice.   What say you then to this device,
  If we dressed up the body of the Duke?
Hippolito. In that disguise of yours?
Vindice.   Y'are quick, y'have reached it.
Hippolito. I like it wondrously.
Vindice. And being in drink, as you have published him,   215
  To lean him on his elbow, as if sleep had caught him,
  Which claims most interest in such sluggy men?
Hippolito. Good yet, but here's a doubt:
  We, thought by th' Duke's son to kill that pander,
  Shall, when he is known, be thought to kill the Duke.   220
Vindice. Neither—O thanks!—It is substantial;

---

202. *There it goes!*] signalling God's judgement, on Vindice as well as Lussurioso; see V.iii.42–3.
  203. *lose*] overreach; but Vindice picks up on the meaning 'lose our way'.
  208. *conveyed*] made away with, disposed of.
  210.] proverbial ('murder will out'); compare V.iii.111–12.
  215. *published*] proclaimed.
  217. *sluggy*] sluggish.
  219–20.] i.e. Lussurioso will think we have killed Piato, but when 'Piato' is discovered to be the Duke in disguise, people will think we have killed the Duke.
  221. *O thanks!*] i.e. thank goodness, I perceive a way out of this difficulty. *substantial*] firmly based.

For that disguise being on him which I wore,
It will be thought I, which he calls the pander, did kill the
Duke, and fled away in his apparel, leaving him so dis-
guised to avoid swift pursuit.   225
Hippolito. Firmer, and firmer.
Vindice.   Nay, doubt not, 'tis in grain;
I warrant it hold colour.
Hippolito.   Let's about it.
Vindice. But by the way, too, now I think on 't, brother,
Let's conjure that base devil out of our mother.

                                                        Exeunt.

[IV. iii]

    Enter the Duchess, *arm in arm with the* Bastard [SPURIO];
    he seemeth lasciviously to [*look on*] *her. After them, enter*
    SUPERVACUO, *running with a rapier; his brother*
    [AMBITIOSO] *stops him.*

Spurio. Madam, unlock yourself; should it be seen,
Your arm would be suspected.
Duchess. Who is 't that dares suspect or this or these?
May not we deal our favours where we please?
Spurio. I'm confident you may.
                                Exeunt [Duchess *and* SPURIO].
Ambitioso.   'Sfoot, brother, hold.   5
Supervacuo. Wouldst let the bastard shame us?
Ambitioso.   Hold, hold, brother;
There's fitter time than now.
Supervacuo.   Now, when I see it?
Ambitioso. 'Tis too much seen already.
Supervacuo.   Seen and known;
The nobler she's, the baser is she grown.
Ambitioso. If she were bent lasciviously, the fault   10
Of mighty women that sleep soft—O death!

---

226. *in grain*] fast dyed; i.e. a sound scheme.
229. *conjure*] exorcise, expel.

IV.iii.3. *or this or these*] either kisses or caresses (recalling III.v.207)?
9.] the higher her status and rank, the more debauched she has become.
10. *bent lasciviously*] given to being wanton.

Must she needs choose such an unequal sinner
To make all worse?
Supervacuo.   A bastard, the Duke's bastard!
Shame heaped on shame!
Ambitioso.   O, our disgrace!
Most women have small waist the world throughout,   15
But their desires are thousand miles about.
Supervacuo. Come, stay not here; let's after, and prevent,
Or else they'll sin faster than we'll repent.   *Exeunt.*

[IV. iv]

Enter VINDICE *and* HIPPOLITO, *bringing out their mother*
[GRATIANA], *one by one shoulder, and the other by the other, with
daggers in their hands.*

Vindice. O thou, for whom no name is bad enough!
Gratiana. What means my sons? What, will you murder me?
Vindice. Wicked, unnatural parent!
Hippolito.   Fiend of women!
Gratiana. O, are sons turned monsters? Help!
Vindice.   In vain.
Gratiana. Are you so barbarous to set iron nipples   5
Upon the breast that gave you suck?
Vindice.   That breast
Is turned to quarlèd poison.
Gratiana. Cut not your days for 't; am not I your mother?
Vindice. Thou dost usurp that title now by fraud,
For in that shell of mother breeds a bawd.   10
Gratiana. A bawd? O name far loathsomer than hell!
Hippolito. It should be so, knew'st thou thy office well.
Gratiana. I hate it.
Vindice. Ah, is 't possible? Thou only? You powers on high,
That women should dissemble when they die!   15

---

12. *unequal*] in rank and blood.

IV.iv.2. *What . . . me?*] recalling the closet scene, *Hamlet*, IV.iii, and here
echoing l. 21.
   5. *iron nipples*] their daggers.
   7. *quarlèd*] curdled?
   8. *Cut*] cut short; another allusion to Exodus 20.12; see II.ii.97 and n.
   12. *office*] duty (as a mother).

Gratiana. Dissemble?

Vindice.   Did not the Duke's son direct
A fellow of the world's condition hither,
That did corrupt all that was good in thee?
Made thee uncivilly forget thyself,
And work our sister to his lust?

Gratiana.   Who, I?   20
That had been monstrous! I defy that man
For any such intent. None lives so pure
But shall be soiled with slander—good son, believe it not.

Vindice. O, I'm in doubt whether I'm myself, or no.
Stay, let me look again upon this face.   25
Who shall be saved when mothers have no grace?

Hippolito. 'Twould make one half-despair.

Vindice.   I was the man;
Defy me now! Let's see, do 't modestly!

Gratiana. O hell unto my soul!

Vindice. In that disguise, I, sent from the Duke's son,   30
Tried you, and found you base metal,
As any villain might have done.

Gratiana.   O no,
No tongue but yours could have bewitched me so.

Vindice. O nimble in damnation, quick in tune!
There is no devil could strike fire so soon.   35
I am confuted in a word.

Gratiana.   O sons,
Forgive me; to myself I'll prove more true.
You that should honour me, I kneel to you.

                              [*Kneels and weeps.*]

Vindice. A mother to give aim to her own daughter!

Hippolito. True, brother; how far beyond nature 'tis,   40
Though many mothers do 't.

Vindice. Nay, an you draw tears once, go you to bed;

---

17. *the world's*] worldly, devoted to material ends.

19. *uncivilly*] barbarously.

26. *grace*] virtue, or God's grace, as at l. 53.

39. *give aim to*] i.e. act as a bawd to; in archery, to guide the aim of someone shooting at a target.

42. *an*] if.

you . . . you] addressing his dagger.

Wet will make iron blush and change to red.
    Brother, it rains; 'twill spoil your dagger, house it.
Hippolito. 'Tis done.   [*They put up their daggers.*]   45
Vindice. I'faith, 'tis a sweet shower, it does much good.
    The fruitful grounds and meadows of her soul
    Has been long dry; pour down, thou blessèd dew.
    Rise, mother; troth, this shower has made you higher.
Gratiana. [*Rising*] O you heavens,   50
    Take this infectious spot out of my soul,
    I'll rinse it in seven waters of mine eyes!
    Make my tears salt enough to taste of grace!
    To weep is to our sex naturally given,
    But to weep truly, that's a gift from heaven.   55
Vindice. Nay, I'll kiss you now; kiss her, brother.
    Let's marry her to our souls, wherein's no lust,
    And honourably love her.
Hippolito.   Let it be.
Vindice. For honest women are so seld and rare,
    'Tis good to cherish those poor few that are.   60
    O you of easy wax, do but imagine,
    Now the disease has left you, how leprously
    That office would have clinged unto your forehead;
    All mothers that had any graceful hue
    Would have worn masks to hide their face at you.   65
    It would have grown to this: at your foul name,
    Green-coloured maids would have turned red with
        shame.
Hippolito. And then our sister, full of hire and baseness.
Vindice. There had been boiling lead again.
    The Duke's son's great concubine, a drab of state,   70

---

51. *infectious*] diseased, infected.
58. *Let it be*] let it be so; agreed.
59. *seld*] uncommon (modern 'seldom').
61. *O you of easy wax*] i.e. O you, our mother, you who are easily corrupted, pliable.
63. *forehead*] see I.ii.4 and n., and *Hamlet*, III.iv.42–4.
67. *Green-coloured*] 'green' as young and inexperienced, and as suffering green-sickness, the anaemic condition that affects teenage girls and gives them pale cheeks.
68. *hire*] payment for services (as a whore).
70.] describing what Gratiana would have made of Castiza.

A cloth o' silver slut, to have her train
Borne up, and her soul trail i' th' dirt—great!
Hippolito. To be miserably great; rich to be
Eternally wretched.
Vindice.   O common madness!
Ask but the thriving'st harlot in cold blood,   75
She'd give the world to make her honour good.
Perhaps you'll say, but only to th' Duke's son
In private; why, she first begins with one
Who afterward to thousand proves a whore:
Break ice in one place, it will crack in more.   80
Gratiana. Most certainly applied.
Hippolito. O brother, you forget our business.
Vindice. And well remembered. Joy's a subtle elf;
I think man's happiest when he forgets himself.
Farewell, once dried, now holy-watered mead;   85
Our hearts wear feathers, that before wore lead.
Gratiana. I'll give you this, that one I never knew
Plead better for, and 'gainst, the devil than you.
Vindice. You make me proud on't.
Hippolito. Commend us in all virtue to our sister.   90
Vindice. Ay, for the love of heaven, to that true maid.
Gratiana. With my best words.
Vindice.   Why, that was motherly said.
                    Exeunt [VINDICE *and* HIPPOLITO].
Gratiana. I wonder now what fury did transport me.
I feel good thoughts begin to settle in me.
O, with what forehead can I look on her,   95
Whose honour I've so impiously beset?
And here she comes.

                    [*Enter* CASTIZA.]

Castiza. Now mother, you have wrought with me so strongly,
That what for my advancement as to calm

80.] marked as a 'sentence' or maxim (see I.i.38).
85. *once . . . mead*] continuing the imagery of lines 46–9.
87. *I'll give you this*] I'll say this for you.
95. *forehead*] as representing impudence, or shame; see II.ii.162–3 and l. 63 above.
99. *what for*] as much for.

The trouble of your tongue, I am content.   100
Gratiana. Content, to what?
Castiza.   To do as you have wished me;
      To prostitute my breast to the Duke's son,
      And put myself to common usury.
Gratiana. I hope you will not so.
Castiza.   Hope you I will not?
      That's not the hope you look to be saved in.   105
Gratiana. Truth, but it is.
Castiza.   Do not deceive yourself;
      I am as you e'en out of marble wrought.
      What would you now? Are ye not pleased yet with me?
      You shall not wish me to be more lascivious
      Than I intend to be.
Gratiana.   Strike not me cold.   110
Castiza. How often have you charged me, on your blessing,
      To be a cursèd woman? When you knew
      Your blessing had no force to make me lewd,
      You laid your curse upon me. That did more;
      The mother's curse is heavy; where that fights,   115
      Suns set in storm, and daughters lose their lights.
Gratiana. Good child, dear maid, if there be any spark
      Of heavenly intellectual fire within thee,
      O, let my breath revive it to a flame;
      Put not all out, with woman's wilful follies.   120
      I am recovered of that foul disease
      That haunts too many mothers. Kind, forgive me;
      Make me not sick in health. If then
      My words prevailed when they were wickedness,
      How much more now when they are just and good!   125
Castiza. I wonder what you mean. Are not you she
      For whose infect persuasions I could scarce

---

103. *usury*] use for profit, or prostitution; see II.ii.99.
107. *out . . . wrought*] i.e. impervious to shame; compare I.iii.8.
109. *shall not*] cannot.
116.] quibbling on 'sons', and on 'lights' as (1) the heavenly bodies, sun,
moon and stars (2) spiritual illumination.
121. *disease*] see I.iii.79 and n.
122. *Kind*] addressing her as both loving, or 'kind one', and 'my child'
('kind' = 'kin').
127. *infect*] tainted.

Kneel out my prayers, and had much ado
In three hours' reading to untwist so much
Of the black serpent as you wound about me?   130
Gratiana. 'Tis unfruitful, held tedious to repeat
What's past; I'm now your present mother.
Castiza. Push, now 'tis too late.
Gratiana.   Bethink again,
Thou know'st not what thou say'st.
Castiza.   No? Deny
Advancement, treasure, the Duke's son?
Gratiana.   O see,   135
I spoke those words, and now they poison me.
What will the deed do then?
Advancement, true; as high as shame can pitch!
For treasure, who e'er knew a harlot rich?
Or could build by the purchase of her sin   140
An hospital to keep their bastards in?
The Duke's son? O, when women are young courtiers,
They are sure to be old beggars:
To know the miseries most harlots taste,
Thou'dst wish thyself unborn when thou art unchaste.   145
Castiza. O mother, let me twine about your neck,
And kiss you till my soul melt on your lips;
I did but this to try you.
Gratiana.   O, speak truth!
Castiza. Indeed, I did but,
For no tongue has force to alter me from honest.   150
If maidens would, men's words could have no power;
A virgin honour is a crystal tower,
Which, being weak, is guarded with good spirits;
Until she basely yields, no ill inherits.

---

133. *Bethink*] consider.
136. *spoke those words*] at II.i.160.
140. *purchase*] profit.
141. *hospital*] orphanage.
149. *I did but*] i.e. I was just testing (repeating what she said in the previous line).
150. *honest*] virtuous.
151. *would*] i.e. would be virtuous.
154. *inherits*] takes possession, dwells there.

Gratiana. O happy child! Faith, and thy birth hath saved me.   155
    'Mongst thousand daughters, happiest of all others,
    Be thou a glass for maids, and I for mothers.   *Exeunt.*

---

157. *glass*] mirror, example.

Act V

Enter VINDICE *and* HIPPOLITO *[with the body of the* Duke *dressed in Vindice's disguise as Piato; they arrange the body to look like a sleeping man].*

Vindice. So, so, he leans well; take heed you wake him not, brother.

Hippolito. I warrant you, my life for yours.

Vindice. That's a good lay, for I must kill myself. Brother, that's I; that sits for me. Do you mark it? And I must 5 stand ready here to make away myself yonder—I must sit to be killed, and stand to kill myself. I could vary it not so little as thrice over again; 't has some eight returns, like Michaelmas term.

Hippolito. That's enow, o' conscience. 10

Vindice. But sirrah, does the Duke's son come single?

Hippolito. No, there's the hell on 't; his faith's too feeble to go alone. He brings flesh-flies after him, that will buzz against supper-time and hum for his coming out.

Vindice. Ah, the fly-flap of vengeance beat 'em to pieces! Here 15 was the sweetest occasion, the fittest hour, to have made my revenge familiar with him; shown him the body of the

---

V.i.3. *my life for yours*] I'll bet my life against yours.

4. *lay*] bet.

5. *that's I*] referring to the Duke's body, dressed as Piato.

6–7. *I must . . . kill myself*] I stand ready to murder 'myself', that is the Duke disguised as Piato, whose body is in a sitting position.

8. *returns*] ways of describing it; properly the reports of a sheriff on writs directed to him by a court of law, and hence the days on which such returns were made; there were eight such days in Michaelmas Term.

10.] That's enough, on my conscience; i.e. don't get carried away.

13. *flesh-flies*] blow-flies, that live on decaying flesh; hence courtiers who live on corruption.

14. *against*] in anticipation of.

15. *the fly-flap*] may the fly-swatter.

121

Duke his father, and how quaintly he died, like a politi-
cian in hugger-mugger, made no man acquainted with it,
and in catastrophe, slain him over his father's breast; and   20
O, I'm mad to lose such a sweet opportunity.

Hippolito. Nay, push, prithee be content; there's no remedy
present. May not hereafter times open in as fair faces as
this?

Vindice. They may, if they can paint so well.   25

Hippolito. Come, now to avoid all suspicion, let's forsake this
room, and be going to meet the Duke's son.

Vindice. Content; I'm for any weather. Heart! Step close, here
he comes.

Enter LUSSURIOSO.

Hippolito. My honoured lord!   30

Lussurioso. O me! You both present?

Vindice. E'en newly, my lord, just as your lordship entered
now. About this place we had notice given he should be,
but in some loathsome plight or other.

Hippolito. Came your honour private?   35

Lussurioso. Private enough for this; only a few
Attend my coming out.

Hippolito. [*Aside*]   Death rot those few!

Lussurioso. Stay, yonder's the slave.

Vindice. Mass, there's the slave indeed, my lord.
[*Aside*]'Tis a good child; he calls his father slave.   40

Lussurioso. Ay, that's the villain, the damned villain. Softly,
Tread easy.

Vindice.   Puh, I warrant you, my lord,
We'll stifle in our breaths.

Lussurioso.   That will do well.—

---

18. *quaintly*] curiously.

19. *in hugger-mugger*] in secret.

20. *in catastrophe*] in conclusion, as at the end of a tragedy.

23–4. *hereafter . . . this*] the future may present as good opportunities as
this.

25. *paint*] i.e. dissemble.

28. *I'm for any weather*] i.e. I'm ready for anything that comes.

33. *About . . . be*] we were told Piato would be somewhere around here.

38. *yonder's the slave*] Lussurioso notices the body, thinking it to be that of
Piato.

43. *stifle in*] hold in, suppress.

Base rogue, thou sleep'st thy last. [*Aside*] 'Tis policy
To have him killed in 's sleep, for if he waked   45
He would betray all to them.

Vindice.   But my lord—

Lussurioso. Ha? What say'st?

Vindice.   Shall we kill him now he's drunk?

Lussurioso. Ay, best of all.

Vindice. Why, then he will ne'er live to be sober.

Lussurioso. No matter, let him reel to hell.   50

Vindice. But being so full of liquor, I fear he will put out all
      the fire.

Lussurioso. Thou art a mad beast.

Vindice. [*Aside*] And leave none to warm your lordship's golls
      withal,—[*Aloud*] for he that dies drunk falls into hellfire   55
      like a bucket o' water, qush, qush.

Lussurioso. Come, be ready, nake your swords, think of your
      wrongs. This slave has injured you.

Vindice. Troth, so he has; [*Aside*] and he has paid well for 't.

Lussurioso. Meet with him now.   60

Vindice. You'll bear us out, my lord?

Lussurioso. Puh, am I a lord for nothing, think you? Quickly
      now.

            [*Vindice and Hippolito stab the Duke's body.*]

Vindice. Sa, sa, sa; thump. There he lies.

Lussurioso. Nimbly done. Ha! O, villains, murderers,
      'Tis the old Duke my father!

Vindice.   That's a jest.   65

Lussurioso. What, stiff and cold already?

51–2. *all the fire*] all the flames of hell.

53.] What a madcap joker you are! Lussurioso is amused by Vindice's
flippancy.

54. *golls*] hands.

56. *qush, qush*] making a splashing sound; compare the modern 'squish'.

57. *nake*] unsheathe (make naked).

58–9. *This slave . . . for 't*] Vindice's private joke is that the 'slave' is really
the Duke, who has paid for the injuries he did with his death, not Piato as
Lussurioso supposes.

60. *Meet with him*] encounter him (as an enemy).

61. *bear us out*] back us up, protect us.

63. *Sa, sa, sa*] a cry used by fencers when making a thrust (from the
French *ça*).

65. *That's a jest*] you must be kidding.

O, pardon me to call you from your names;
'Tis none of your deed.—That villain Piato,
Whom you thought now to kill, has murdered him,
And left him thus disguised.

Hippolito.   And not unlikely.   70

Vindice. O rascal! Was he not ashamed
To put the Duke into a greasy doublet?

Lussurioso. He has been cold and stiff, who knows how long?

Vindice. [*Aside*] Marry, that do I!

Lussurioso. No words, I pray, of anything intended.   75

Vindice. O, my lord.

Hippolito. I would fain have your lordship think that we have
small reason to prate.

Lussurioso. Faith, thou say'st true. I'll forthwith send to court
For all the nobles, bastard, Duchess, all;   80
How here, by miracle, we found him dead,
And in his raiment that foul villain fled.

Vindice. That will be the best way, my lord, to clear us all;
let's cast about to be clear.

Lussurioso. Ho, Nencio, Sordido, and the rest.   85

Enter all [his followers, among them SORDIDO *and* NENCIO].

Sordido. My lord.

Nencio. My lord.

Lussurioso. Be witnesses of a strange spectacle:
Choosing for private conference that sad room,
We found the Duke my father gealed in blood.   90

Sordido. My lord the Duke?—Run, hie thee, Nencio;
Startle the court by signifying so much.   [*Exit* NENCIO.]

Vindice. [*Aside*] Thus much by wit a deep revenger can,
When murder's known, to be the clearest man.
We're furthest off, and with as bold an eye   95

---

67. *from your names*] i.e. by names that wrong you ('villains, murderers', l.
64).

75.] i.e. don't say a word about my commissioning you to kill Piato.

76.] i.e. of course I won't.

82.] and the foul villain Piato has fled disguised in the Duke's clothes.

90. *gealed*] congealed.

93. *can*] can do.

94. *clearest*] most free from suspicion.

Survey his body as the standers-by.
Lussurioso. My royal father, too basely let blood
   By a malevolent slave.
Hippolito. [*Aside to Vindice*]   Hark,
   He calls thee slave again.
Vindice. [*Aside to Hippolito*]   'Has lost, he may.
Lussurioso. O sight! Look hither, see, his lips are gnawn   100
   With poison.
Vindice.   How, his lips? By th' mass, they be.
Lussurioso. O villain! O rogue! O slave! O rascal!
Hippolito. [*Aside to Vindice*] O good deceit; he quits him
      with like terms!

[*Enter* Nobles, *preceding* AMBITIOSO *and* SUPERVACUO.]

1. Noble. Where?
2. Noble. Which way?   105
Ambitioso. Over what roof hangs this prodigious comet
   In deadly fire?
Lussurioso.   Behold, behold, my lords,
   The Duke my father's murdered by a vassal
   That owes this habit, and here left disguised.

[*Enter* Duchess *and* SPURIO.]

Duchess. My lord and husband!   110
2. Noble. Reverend majesty!
1. Noble.   I have seen these clothes
   Often attending on him.
Vindice. [*Aside to Hippolito*]   That nobleman
   Has been i' th' country, for he does not lie.
Supervacuo. [*To Ambitioso*] Learn of our mother, let's
      dissemble too;
   I am glad he's vanished—so, I hope, are you?   115

---

99. *'Has lost, he may*] he has lost the combat between us, so I don't mind
if he calls me 'slave' now.

103. *quits . . . terms*] requites him with terms like those the Duke used
against Lussurioso at II.iii.15.

106-7. *Over . . . fire?*] Ambitioso asks, in effect, 'Where is this ominous
and frightening sight?', or 'What dreadful destiny is hanging over us?' A
comet appears in V.iii.

109. *owes this habit*] owns this suit of clothes.

113.] Truth was proverbially found in the country, and duplicity at court.

Ambitioso. [*To Supervacuo*] Ay, you may take my word for 't.
Spurio. [*Aside*]   Old dad dead?
    I, one of his cast sins, will send the fates
    Most hearty commendations by his own son;
    I'll tug in the new stream till strength be done.
Lussurioso. Where be those two that did affirm to us   120
    My lord the Duke was privately rid forth?
1. Noble. O, pardon us, my lords; he gave that charge
    Upon our lives, if he were missed at court,
    To answer so. He rode not anywhere;
    We left him private with that fellow here.   125
Vindice. [*Aside*] Confirmed.
Lussurioso.   O heavens, that false charge was his death!
    Impudent beggars! Durst you to our face
    Maintain such a false answer? Bear him straight
    To execution.
1. Noble.   My lord!
Lussurioso.   Urge me no more.
    In this, the excuse may be called half the murder.   130
Vindice. You've sentenced well.
Lussurioso.   Away, see it be done.
                    [*Exit* First Noble, *guarded.*]
Vindice. [*Aside*] Could you not stick? See what confession
        doth!
    Who would not lie, when men are hanged for
        truth?
Hippolito. [*Aside to Vindice*] Brother, how happy is our venge-
        ance!
Vindice. [*Aside to Hippolito*]   Why, it hits
    Past the apprehension of indifferent wits.   135

---

117. *cast*] discarded.

117–18. *will . . . son*] i.e. will kill Lussurioso and send hearty greetings by means of him to the goddesses of destiny.

119. *tug*] contend (from 'tug' = pull at an oar).

till . . . done] as long as my strength holds out.

122. *charge*] command.

126. *Confirmed*] Vindice's story is confirmed, and others appear guilty of the Duke's murder.

132. *Could . . . stick?*] Vindice is speaking as though to the condemned nobleman: 'Didn't you have sense enough to keep silent?'

134–5. *it hits . . . wits*] i.e. it comes off, succeeds, better than people of common understanding could appreciate.

Lussurioso. My lord, let post-horse be sent into all places to
    entrap the villain.
Vindice. [*Aside*] Post-horse, ha, ha!
2. *Noble.* My lord, we're something bold to know our duty.
    Your father's accidentally departed;   140
    The titles that were due to him meet you.
Lussurioso. Meet me? I'm not at leisure, my good lord.
    I've many griefs to dispatch out o' th' way:—
    [*Aside*] Welcome, sweet titles! [*To them*] Talk to me, my
        lords,
    Of sepulchres and mighty emperors' bones;   145
    That's thought for me.
Vindice. [*Aside*]   So one may see by this
    How foreign markets go:
    Courtiers have feet o' th' nines, and tongues o' th'
        twelves;
    They flatter dukes, and dukes flatter themselves.
2. *Noble.* [*To Lussurioso*] My lord, it is your shine must com-
    fort us.   150
Lussurioso. Alas, I shine in tears, like the sun in April.
Sordido. You're now my lord's grace.
Lussurioso. My lord's grace? I perceive you'll have it so.
Sordido. 'Tis but your own.
Lussurioso. Then heavens give me grace to be so.   155
Vindice. [*Aside*] He prays well for himself.
3. *Noble.* [*To the Duchess*]   Madam, all sorrows
    Must run their circles into joys. No doubt but time
    Will make the murderer bring forth himself.
Vindice. [*Aside*] He were an ass then, i'faith.
3. *Noble.*   In the mean season,
    Let us bethink the latest funeral honours   160

---

    136. *post-horse*] couriers on horseback.

    139. *we're . . . duty*] we are rather eager to know where our obedience lies.

    146–7. *So . . . go*] Vindice's point seems to be that as the new Duke
behaves, so his courtiers will follow suit; perhaps a comment too for an
English audience?—this is how people behave abroad.

    148. *feet . . . twelves*] i.e. their (flattering) mouths are three sizes larger than
their feet.

    149. *flatter themselves*] deceive themselves.

    154. *but your own*] merely what is due to you.

    156–7. *all . . . joys*] all sorrows eventually give way to joys.

    160–1. *Let . . . Due*] let us consider what final funeral honours are due.

Due to the Duke's cold body—and, withal,
Calling to memory our new happiness
Spread in his royal son. Lords, gentlemen,
Prepare for revels.

Vindice. [*Aside*] Revels?

3. Noble.   Time hath several falls;   165
Griefs lift up joys, feasts put down funerals.

Lussurioso. Come then, my lords; my favours to you all.
[*Aside*] The Duchess is suspected foully bent;
I'll begin dukedom with her banishment!

                            Exeunt LUSSURIOSO, Nobles, *and* Duchess.

Hippolito. [*To Vindice*] Revels!

Vindice. [*To Hippolito*]   Ay, that's the word; we are firm yet.   170
Strike one strain more, and then we crown our wit.

                            Exeunt VINDICE *and* HIPPOLITO.

Spurio. [*Aside*] Well, have at the fairest mark!—so said the
Duke when he begot me—
And if I miss his heart, or near about,
Then have at any; a bastard scorns to be out.   [*Exit.*]   175

Supervacuo. Note'st thou that Spurio, brother?

Ambitioso. Yes, I note him to our shame.

Supervacuo. He shall not live, his hair shall not grow much
longer; in this time of revels, tricks may be set afoot.
See'st thou yon new moon? It shall outlive the new duke   180
by much; this hand shall dispossess him, then we're
mighty.
A masque is treason's licence, that build upon;

---

163. *son*] and 'sun', spreading happiness.

165. *Time . . . falls*] i.e. the times keep changing; 'falls' may mean (1)
collars (2) overthrows, as in wrestling (3) seasons of decline (autumns).

166.] griefs give way to and enhance joy, and feasts get rid of the sadness
of funerals.

168. *bent*] inclined.

170. *firm*] secure.

171. *Strike one strain*] play one tune (but with suggestion of striking a
blow).

172. *mark*] target (i.e. Lussurioso).

175. *out*] out of the action.

180–1. *It . . . much*] i.e. long before the month is out Lussurioso will be
dead.

183. *masque*] a dance by men disguised and masked, a common entertainment at feasts; masques developed into elaborate entertainments at the
Jacobean court.

that build upon] base your plans on that.

'Tis murder's best face when a vizard's on.   *Exit.*
Ambitioso. Is 't so? 'Tis very good.   185
    And do you think to be duke then, kind brother?
    I'll see fair play; drop one, and there lies t'other.   *Exit.*

[v. ii]

    Enter VINDICE *and* HIPPOLITO *with* PIERO *and other* Nobles.

Vindice. My lords, be all of music; strike old griefs
    Into other countries
    That flow in too much milk and have faint livers,
    Not daring to stab home their discontents.
    Let our hid flames break out, as fire, as lightning,   5
    To blast this villainous dukedom vexed with sin;
    Wind up your souls to their full height again.
Piero. How?
1. Noble.   Which way?
2. Noble.   Any way; our wrongs are such,
    We cannot justly be revenged too much.
Vindice. You shall have all enough;—revels are toward,   10
    And those few nobles that have long suppressed you
    Are busied to the furnishing of a masque,
    And do affect to make a pleasant tale on 't;
    The masquing suits are fashioning. Now comes in
    That which must glad us all—we to take pattern   15
    Of all those suits, the colour, trimming, fashion,
    E'en to an undistinguished hair almost;
    Then, ent'ring first, observing the true form,

    V.ii.1. *music; strike*] see V.i.171 and n.
    3. *flow . . . milk*] are not manly enough.
    have faint livers] lack courage; quibbling on 'livers' = people, inhabitants.
    4. *home*] all the way.
    7.] i.e. brace yourselves for action. The image seems to be derived from tightening the screw on a crossbow, or possibly the pegs on a stringed musical instrument.
    10. *toward*] in preparation.
    12. *busied to*] busied about.
    13. *affect*] aim.
    tale] fiction or allegory.
    14. *fashioning*] being made.
    15. *take pattern*] copy the pattern.
    17. *undistinguished hair*] exact (indistinguishable) detail.
    18. *form*] order of the dance.

Within a strain or two we shall find leisure
To steal our swords out handsomely,   20
And when they think their pleasure sweet and good,
In midst of all their joys, they shall sigh blood.
Piero. Weightily, effectually.
3. Noble. Before the t' other maskers come—
Vindice. We're gone, all done and past.   25
Piero. But how for the Duke's guard?
Vindice.   Let that alone;
By one and one their strengths shall be drunk down.
Hippolito. There are five hundred gentlemen in the action,
That will apply themselves, and not stand idle.
Piero. O, let us hug your bosoms!
Vindice.   Come, my lords,   30
Prepare for deeds, let other times have words.   *Exeunt.*

[v.iii]

In a dumb show, the possessing of the young Duke [LUSSURIOSO]
with all his Nobles; *then sounding music. A furnished table is brought
forth; then enters the* Duke *and his* Nobles *to the banquet. A blazing
star appeareth.*

1. Noble. Many harmonious hours and choicest pleasures
Fill up the royal numbers of your years.
Lussurioso. My lords, we're pleased to thank you,—though we
know
'Tis but your duty now to wish it so.
1. Noble. That shine makes us all happy.
3. Noble [*Aside*]   His grace frowns.   5
2. Noble. [*Aside*] Yet we must say he smiles.
1. Noble. [*Aside*]   I think we must.

---

19. *strain*] i.e. of music.
26. *Let that alone*] don't worry about that.
27. *their . . . down*] i.e. they will be overcome by being made drunk.

V.iii.0.1–2. dumb . . . *Nobles*] i.e. the installation of Lussurioso (in robes
and coronet) as duke is mimed, with the nobles doing homage.
0.3–4. blazing star] How such a flare (l. 19) was managed is not known,
but it was an established effect in the public theatres.
4.] your duty obliges you to say that.
5. *shine*] ironic if, as it appears, no one notices the 'star' until l. 15.

Lussurioso. [*Aside*] That foul, incontinent Duchess we have
　　banished;
　　The bastard shall not live. After these revels,
　　I'll begin strange ones; he and the stepsons
　　Shall pay their lives for the first subsidies.　　　　　　　　10
　　We must not frown so soon, else 't had been now.
1. Noble. My gracious lord, please you prepare for pleasure;
　　The masque is not far off.
Lussurioso.　　　　　　　　We are for pleasure.
　　　　　　　　　　　　　　[*Noticing the blazing star*]
　　Beshrew thee, what art thou? Thou made'st me start!
　　Thou hast committed treason:—a blazing star!　　　　　　15
1. Noble. A blazing star? O, where, my lord?
Lussurioso.　　　　　　　　　　Spy out.
2. Noble. See, see, my lords, a wondrous dreadful one.
Lussurioso. I am not pleased at that ill-knotted fire,
　　That bushing, flaring star,—am not I duke?
　　It should not quake me now. Had it appeared　　　　　　20
　　Before, it I might then have justly feared;
　　But yet they say, whom art and learning weds,
　　When stars wear locks they threaten great men's heads.
　　Is it so? You are read, my lords.
1. Noble.　　　　　　　　May it please your grace,
　　It shows great anger.
Lussurioso.　　　　That does not please our grace.　　　25
2. Noble. Yet here's the comfort, my lord: many times,
　　When it seems most, it threatens farthest off.
Lussurioso. Faith, and I think so, too.
1. Noble.　　　　　　　　Beside, my lord,

---

　　10. *subsidies*] instalments (properly money granted to the sovereign for
special needs, usually in the form of taxes).
　　11.] i.e. I must not move too fast, or I would have them executed now.
　　14–15.] First seeing the 'star' as a stage effect in the masque, he then
realises it is 'real', and an omen of death (see V.i.106, and l. 23 below).
　　19. *bushing*] like a comet's tail.
　　20. *quake*] cause to tremble.
　　22. *whom . . . weds*] i.e. those who combine skill and learning.
　　23. *wear locks*] i.e. are comets (have a trail of 'hair').
　　24. *read*] learned.
　　25. *our grace*] sardonically echoing the conventional phrase, 'May it please
your grace', l. 24.
　　27. *most*] greatest, most near.

You're gracefully established, with the loves
Of all your subjects; and for natural death,   30
I hope it will be threescore years a-coming.

Lussurioso. True? No more but threescore years?

1. Noble. Fourscore I hope, my lord.

2. Noble.   And fivescore, I.

3. Noble. But 'tis my hope, my lord, you shall ne'er die.

Lussurioso. [*To 3. Noble*] Give me thy hand, these others I
     rebuke;   35
He that hopes so is fittest for a duke;
Thou shalt sit next me.—Take your places, lords;
We're ready now for sports, let 'em set on.—
You thing, we shall forget you quite anon!

3. Noble. I hear 'em coming, my lord.

Enter the masque of revengers, the two brothers [VINDICE *and*
HIPPOLITO], *and two* Lords *more.*

Lussurioso. [*Aside*]   Ah, 'tis well;   40
Brothers, and bastard, you dance next in hell.

The revengers dance;
at the end, steal out their swords, and these four kill the four
at the table in their chairs. It thunders.

Vindice. Mark, thunder! Dost know thy cue, thou big-voiced
     cryer?
Dukes' groans are thunder's watchwords.

Hippolito.   So, my lords,
You have enough.

Vindice.   Come, let's away; no ling'ring.

Hippolito. Follow. Go!   *Exeunt* [*all the maskers but* VINDICE].   45

Vindice. No power is angry when the lustful die;
When thunder claps, heaven likes the tragedy.   *Exit.*

---

30. *for*] as for.

36. *fittest*] i.e. fittest adviser and companion.

38. *sports*] entertainment.

39. *thing*] the 'comet', still visible; or possibly the First Noble, who displeased Lussurioso at ll. 25 and 30–1.

41.2. these four kill the four] i.e., Vindice and Hippolito, with two lords, in the masque or dance of revengers, kill Lussurioso and three noblemen who are sitting at a table.

41.3. thunders] the voice of God in, for example, Job 40.4; see IV.ii.202.

47. *claps*] suggesting applause from heaven.

Lussurioso. O, O!

> *Enter the other masque of intended murderers, stepsons*
> [AMBITIOSO *and* SUPERVACUO], Bastard [SPURIO], *and a*
> Fourth Man, *coming in dancing. The* Duke [LUSSURIOSO]
> *recovers a little in voice, and groans—calls, 'A guard! Treason!'*
> *At which, they all start out of their measure, and turning*
> *towards the table, they find them all to be murdered.*

Spurio. Whose groan was that?
Lussurioso. Treason! A guard!
Ambitioso.   How now, all murdered?
Supervacuo.   Murdered!   50
4. Noble. And those his nobles!
Ambitioso.   Here's a labour saved,
   I thought to have sped him. 'Sblood, how came this?
Supervacuo. Then I proclaim myself; now I am duke.
Ambitioso. Thou duke? Brother, thou liest.
                         [*Stabs Supervacuo.*]
Spurio.   Slave, so dost thou.
                         [*Stabs Ambitioso.*]
4. Noble. Base villain, hast thou slain my lord and master?   55
                         [*Stabs Spurio.*]

> *Enter* [VINDICE, HIPPOLITO, *and the other*] *first masquers.*

Vindice. Pistols! Treason! Murder! Help, guard my lord
   The Duke.

> [*Enter* ANTONIO *with a* Guard.]

Hippolito.   Lay hold upon this traitor!
                 [*The Guard seizes the Fourth Noble.*]
Lussurioso.   O!
Vindice. Alas, the Duke is murdered.
Hippolito.   And the nobles.
Vindice. Surgeons, surgeons! [*Aside*] Heart, does he breathe
   so long?
Antonio. A piteous tragedy, able to make   60

   48.5. measure] dance.
   52. sped] killed.
   57.SD. Enter ANTONIO] Antonio at once takes charge, now the Duke is
dead, the Duchess banished (V.i.169), and their sons are all dead.

An old man's eyes bloodshot.

Lussurioso. O!

Vindice. Look to my lord the Duke. [*Aside*] A vengeance
   throttle him!—

   [*To 4. Noble*] Confess, thou murderous and unhallowed
      man,

   Didst thou kill all these?

4. Noble.   None but the bastard, I.   65

Vindice. How came the Duke slain, then?

4. Noble.   We found him so.

Lussurioso. O, villain!—

Vindice. Hark!

Lussurioso.   —Those in the masque did murder us.

Vindice. La you now, sir;—

   [*To 4. Noble*] O marble impudence! Will you confess
      now?   70

4. Noble. 'Sblood, 'tis all false.

Antonio.   Away with that foul monster,

   Dipped in a prince's blood.

4. Noble.   Heart, 'tis a lie!

Antonio. Let him have bitter execution.

                            [*Exit the* Fourth Noble, *guarded.*]

Vindice. New marrow! No, I cannot be expressed.

   How fares my lord the Duke?

Lussurioso.   Farewell to all;   75

   He that climbs highest has the greatest fall.

   My tongue is out of office.

Vindice.   Air, gentlemen, air!

   [*Whispering in his ear*] Now thou'lt not prate on 't, 'twas
      Vindice murdered thee,—

Lussurioso. O!

Vindice.   —murdered thy father,—

Lussurioso.   O!   [*Dies.*]

Vindice.   —and I am he.

   Tell nobody. [*To the others*] So, so, the Duke's departed. 80

Antonio. It was a deadly hand that wounded him;

---

   69. *La you*] a common exclamation.

   74. *marrow*] food (for his revenge).

   be expressed] put my feelings into words.

The rest, ambitious who should rule and sway,
After his death were so made all away.
Vindice. My lord was unlikely.
Hippolito.   Now the hope
Of Italy lies in your reverend years.   85
Vindice. Your hair will make the silver age again,
When there was fewer but more honest men.
Antonio. The burden's weighty, and will press age down;
May I so rule that heaven may keep the crown.
Vindice. The rape of your good lady has been quited   90
With death on death.
Antonio.   Just is the law above!
But, of all things, it puts me most to wonder
How the old Duke came murdered.
Vindice.   O, my lord.
Antonio. It was the strangeliest carried, I not heard of the like.
Hippolito. 'Twas all done for the best, my lord.   95
Vindice. All for your grace's good. We may be bold to speak it
now; 'twas somewhat witty carried, though we say it.
'Twas we two murdered him.
Antonio. You two?
Vindice. None else, i'faith, my lord; nay, 'twas well managed.   100
Antonio. Lay hands upon those villains.
                    [*The Guard seize Vindice and Hippolito.*]
Vindice.   How? on us?
Antonio. Bear 'em to speedy execution.
Vindice. Heart, was 't not for your good, my lord?
Antonio.   My good?
Away with 'em! Such an old man as he;
You that would murder him would murder me.   105

---

82. *The rest*] i.e. the Duchess's sons, Ambitioso, Supervacuo and Spurio.
83. *so*] similarly.
84. *unlikely*] unfit (to be duke).
85. *your*] Antonio's.
86. *silver age*] see IV.i.35 and n.
89. *keep*] protect.
90. *quited*] paid for.
94. *carried*] managed.
97. *witty carried*] cleverly contrived.
104. *Such . . . he*] i.e. he was an old man much like myself.

Vindice. Is 't come about?

Hippolito.   'Sfoot, brother, you begun.

Vindice. May not we set as well as the Duke's son?
　Thou hast no conscience; are we not revenged?
　Is there one enemy left alive amongst those?
　'Tis time to die, when we are ourselves our foes.   110
　When murd'rers shut deeds close, this curse does seal
　　'em:
　If none disclose 'em, they themselves reveal 'em.
　This murder might have slept in tongueless brass
　But for ourselves, and the world died an ass.

　Now I remember, too, here was Piato brought forth a   115
　knavish sentence once; no doubt, said he, but time will
　make the murderer bring forth himself. 'Tis well he died,
　he was a witch.

　And now, my lord, since we are in for ever,
　This work was ours, which else might have been slipped,   120
　And, if we list, we could have nobles clipped
　And go for less than beggars; but we hate
　To bleed so cowardly. We have enough, i'faith;
　We're well, our mother turned, our sister true;
　We die after a nest of dukes. Adieu.   125

　　　　　　　Exeunt [VINDICE *and* HIPPOLITO, *guarded*].

---

106. *Is 't come about?*] has our luck (literally, the wind, see IV.i.37) changed?

107. *son*] or sun (which can 'set' or decline); see IV.iv.116.

108. *conscience*] sense of what is right.

111–17. *When . . . himself*] varying maxims like 'Murder will out' (see IV.ii.210), and 'Time brings truth to light'.

113. *brass*] i.e. a brass plaque, commonly placed in churches to commemmorate the dead.

114. *and . . . ass*] i.e. and the world remained in ignorance.

115. *brought*] who brought.

116. *sentence*] saying.

118. *witch*] because he could prophesy.

119. *are in*] are involved in the business.

120. *been slipped*] passed unnoticed.

121. *nobles clipped*] the noblemen in the plot beheaded; but playing on 'nobles' = gold coins, often clipped, or mutilated, and so reduced in value.

124. *turned*] converted.

Antonio. How subtilly was that murder closed! Bear up
   Those tragic bodies; 'tis a heavy season.
   Pray heaven their blood may wash away all treason!

                                        Exeunt.

        FINIS.

---

126. *closed*] kept secret.